SAM
STEELE

Also by Norman S. Leach

*Cavalry of the Air: An Illustrated
Introduction to the Aircraft and Aces of
the First World War*

SAM STEELE

AN OFFICER AND A GENTLEMAN

Norman S. Leach

DUNDURN
TORONTO

Note: In some cases, the print quality of images in this book has been affected by
the age and condition of original material.

Copy Editor: Kat Mototsune
Interior Design: BJ Weckerle
Cover Design: Carmen Giraudy
Cover Image: Sam Steele (1918). Bruce Peel Special Collections Library,
University of Alberta (2008.1.3.3.6.1.1)
Printer: Webcom

Library and Archives Canada Cataloguing in Publication

Leach, Norman, 1963-, author
Sam Steele : an officer and a gentleman / Norman S. Leach.

Issued in print and electronic formats.
ISBN 978-1-4597-2827-1 (pbk.).—ISBN 978-1-4597-2828-8 (pdf).--
ISBN 978-1-4597-2829-5 (epub)

1. Steele, Samuel B. (Samuel Benfield), 1848–1919.
2. North West Mounted Police (Canada)—Biography. 3. Police—Canada, Western—Biography.
4. Northwest, Canadian—History. 5. Canada—History—1867–1914. I. Title.

FC3216.3.S77L42 2014   363.2092   C2014-905038-0
                                            C2014-905039-9

1 2 3 4 5   19 18 17 16 15

We acknowledge the support of the **Canada Council for the Arts** and the **Ontario Arts Council**
for our publishing program. We also acknowledge the financial support of the **Government of Canada**
through the **Canada Book Fund** and **Livres Canada Books**, and the **Government of Ontario** through
the **Ontario Book Publishing Tax Credit** and the **Ontario Media Development Corporation**.

Care has been taken to trace the ownership of copyright material used in this book.
The author and the publisher welcome any information enabling them to rectify any references
or credits in subsequent editions.
J. Kirk Howard, President

The publisher is not responsible for websites or their content unless they are owned by the publisher.

Printed and bound in Canada.

VISIT US AT

Dundurn.com | *@dundurnpress* | *Facebook.com/dundurnpress* | *Pinterest.com/dundurnpress*

Dundurn
3 Church Street, Suite 500
Toronto, Ontario, Canada
M5E 1M2

This book is dedicated to the memory of Dennis Johnson —
my colleague, my editor, and my friend.

Foreword

Major-General Sir Sam Steele (1848–1919), mounted policeman, militiaman, and soldier, was one of Canada's great soldier-heroes. From the Fenian Raid of 1866 through the Riel Rebellion, the Boer War, and the First World War, Steele was an iconic figure, serving in all of Canada's major military campaigns, as well as policing western Canada during the building of the Canadian Pacific Railway and the Yukon's Klondike gold rush.

A keen observer of his surroundings, particularly of First Nations peoples as they adjusted to ever-encroaching settlement, Steele left a record of his life on patrol and campaign in official documents, hundreds of letters to his wife, thousands of pages of diaries, and hundreds of photographs. Potentially a major historical resource, the Steele papers were privately held by Steele's descendants and inaccessible for ninety years.

The Steele Family Crest.

The Sir Samuel Benfield Steele Collection is a Canadian national treasure. Since its acquisition in 2008, it has become a major focus of scholarly research activity at the University of Alberta's Bruce Peel Special Collections Library (*http://steele.library.ualberta.ca* provides descriptions of the Collection). The Steele papers are providing historians and biographers with fresh insights into the settlement and development of the Canadian West (including the Yukon), the North-West Mounted Police, and Canada's major military campaigns at home and abroad.

This admirably readable and handsomely illustrated biography of Steele by eminent Calgary author Norman Leach is a fine example of these endeavours to revise and enrich the Canadian historical tapestry.

Dr. Merrill Distad
Associate University Librarian (Research & Special Collections Services) and University Archivist, University of Alberta, Edmonton
December 2013

Acknowledgements

Very special thanks to:

Lynda Whiston, Collections Manager, Orillia Museum of Art and History, Orillia, Ontario

Murray Cayley, Orillia, Ontario

Jamie Hunter, Director, Huronia Museum, Midland, Ontario

Findlay Johnson Payne, Victoria, British Columbia

Joan L. Hyslop, Registrar, Grey Roots Museum & Archives, Owen Sound, Ontario

All my love and gratitude to my wife Maritza and my daughters Stephanie and Chelsea who allow me to follow my passion for military history.

Prologue

A Man of Judgement in Unsettled Times

The elders of Clarksburg, Ontario, must have felt sheepish as they assembled in Turnbull's Store in the late spring of 1866. They milled about, embarrassed to come to the point. Finally they approached eighteen-year-old store clerk Sam Steele with an unusual request. Would he take command of the local militia company that he had raised and trained?

Under normal circumstances it would be unthinkable to ask one so young to lead troops, but 1866 was not a normal time in the British colony of Canada. The Civil War in the United States had drawn to a close the year before. Across America well-trained soldiers were being released from military duties to return to their shops and farms. Many were able to hang up the tools of war and return to a quiet life — others continued to crave the action of combat.

For the Fenian Brotherhood, a group dedicated to the liberation of Ireland from British rule, the bored combat veterans were a huge asset. The Fenians launched a secret plan to invade Canada using American ex-soldiers who supported the liberation of Ireland. The Fenian leadership in the United States believed that such an attack would encourage Irish loyalists living in Canada to rise up in solidarity, and that Britain's hold on Canada would be threatened. The British, fearing the loss of their valuable colony, would move troops from Great Britain (including Ireland) to put down the rebellion. With fewer British troops in Ireland, the American Fenians believed their brethren in Ireland would be able to oust the British. All very simple — on paper.

The American government had a law against Americans fighting in foreign wars, but there was some belief in Canada that the United States was ignoring the growing Fenian threat. While some of the conspirators were arrested south of the border in 1866, the Fenians remained confident enough to put their plan into action.

Many Irish Canadians were torn by their loyalties between Ireland and Canada and, for the most part, stayed out of the fight. For others in Canada, it was clear that the country was under attack and needed to be defended. The Clarksburg community delegation knew that Sam Steele possessed the formal and personal qualifications to command. He had graduated at the head of his class in British Army officer-training courses (scoring 100 percent), and he had demonstrated his leadership by mustering the Clarksburg Company of the 31st Canadian Militia Regiment.

The townspeople knew that if ever a boy had been born to command, that boy was Sam Steele. The son of a distinguished British naval captain, his childhood had been spent leading his cousins and younger brothers on endless excursions through woodlands and waterways that had only a few years before been wilderness unexplored by Europeans. He was lean, muscled, and tall, skilled in arts of the frontiersman; he had a sure aim with a rifle, confident command of a horse, and proven physical strength and mental stamina. Sam also had more military experience than most in the area. He had received his commission with Number 6 Company of the 35th Regiment after qualifying with the 2nd Battalion of the Leicestershire Regiment, both British regiments stationed in Canada. He was the natural choice to lead the fighting force he had raised and trained.

Sam turned down the Clarksburg elders — politely but firmly — telling them that an older militia member should be appointed captain of the company. The elders left disappointed but even more impressed with this plain-talking, self-effacing young man whose judgement outstripped his years. Sam Steele had a head on his shoulders.

ONE

The Making of a Hero

A drawing of the Steele family home built by Sam's father, Elmes Yelverton Steele, a veteran of the British Royal Navy (1832).

S am Steele's father, Elmes Yelverton Steele, enjoyed a long and colourful career, first as a British naval officer and then as a Canadian farmer, politician, and civic and military leader. He was born in 1780 at Coleford, Gloucestershire, England, the son of a doctor and one of six brothers to serve in the Royal Navy and British Army. Elmes rose through the ranks, eventually making captain in the world's most powerful navy, a force that projected British colonial rule around the globe.

In 1809 Elmes married Elizabeth Seeley Coucher, and they had six children. After the Napoleonic Wars, Elmes retired from the service and settled his family in France, only to return to England in 1830 at the start of the French Revolution. When retired British military offi-cers were offered grants of free land in Upper Canada, Elmes, then aged fifty-one, immigrated with his son John. He settled in 1832 on a 400-hectare farm in the pioneer community of Fair Valley, near present-day Orillia. Elizabeth and all but one of the children arrived the following year, once Elmes had broken some land and built a spacious home. Elmes named the family estate Purbrook after his wife's birth-place in England.

Elmes was an adventurer and leader who did nothing in a small way. He quickly established himself as a leading citizen by serving as a magis-trate and as lieutenant-colonel of the local militia. He raised a volunteer force to help suppress the abortive Upper Canada Rebellion of 1837, when rebels took up arms against the corrupt colonial elite disparag-ingly known as the "Family Compact." Elmes later spoke out against the abuses and cronyism of the Compact and was elected in 1841 to the Legislative Assembly as a reformer. To improve commerce and civil defence, he lobbied successfully for the construction of the first road connecting Toronto with Orillia and of the Trent Valley Canal portion of the Trent–Severn Waterway.

Elizabeth died in 1846, and Elmes remarried the following year to Anne Johnston, whose family had recently emigrated from Scotland. Elmes was sixty-six; Anne a mere seventeen. The newlyweds wasted no time starting a family, with their first child arriving nine months and three days after the nuptials. Samuel Benfield Steele was born January 5, 1848. Anne went on to bear five more children in the next eleven years.

Sam inherited his father's fondness for command and love of adven-ture. He swam, skated, canoed, and fished the lakes and streams; he

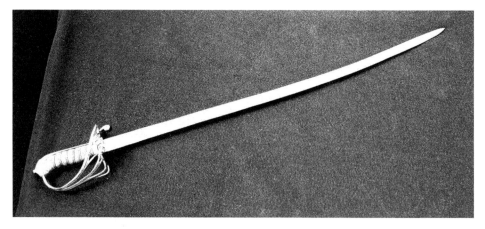

Elmes Steele was very proud of his service in the Royal Navy and his sword still survives. Sam credited his father for his love for military things.

Print of Lake Couchiching near the Steeles' home.

Print of Orillia on Lake Couchiching. Sam spent his formative years in Orillia and in the woods surrounding the village.

hiked and hunted the fields and forests. Almost from the moment he could shoulder a rifle and ride a horse, he was regarded as an accomplished marksman and horseman. Everything Sam did, he did hard.

When Sam was eight or nine years old, the Steele family moved to the nearby settlement of Orillia in the middle of the school year in order for the children to attend school. Though Sam's early years were a rural idyll, his conventional schooling had not been neglected. His father was highly educated and had brought to Fair Valley an ample library and a zeal for learning. He tutored his children and encouraged Sam to take to books as readily as to the arts of bushcraft. Classic adventure stories and Elmes' swashbuckling tales of life on the high seas stirred Sam's imagination. When he entered school in town, Sam advanced quickly to the upper grades.

Then childhood's innocence was lost forever. In 1859, when Sam was only eleven, his mother died of tuberculosis. Much later in life, Sam recalled the years following her death as "filled with much sorrow." Not long after, his father returned permanently to Purbrook, the family estate in Fair Valley, leaving Sam in the care of his much older half-brother John, who had emerged as a community leader and skilled frontiersman. For his whole life, Sam never forgot John's strong but caring mentoring.

Taken in 1850, the relatively new art of photography captures Sam as a baby on his mother's knee. In later years Sam claimed the woman in the photo was actually a neighbour.

Six years later, in August 1865, Sam's father died at age eighty-five. That same year, Sam's sister Elizabeth Jane also died. Given Sam's close bond with his half-brother John and his younger siblings, he was far from being alone in the world, but he must have felt compelled to take stock of his life.

The Fenian menace was only one reason for the colonies of Canada (Ontario and Quebec), New Brunswick, and Nova Scotia to form a confederation to improve security and expand trade. Many feared America's rapid territorial annexation in the continent's south and west would ultimately turn

Canada was a rough and tumble place for kids in 1864. A barrel provides a distraction in this photo of Mississauga.

Sam and his family regularly attended the Fair Valley Church.

The earliest known photo of Sam Steele in a military uniform. It was taken in 1866 as the country prepared for the Fenian raids. Over the years Sam had hundreds of photos taken in a multitude of uniforms.

north, especially as British colonial policy was against maintaining a large defence force in its North American outpost. Everyone was debating the pending union of the colonies into the Dominion of Canada. Sam had found a passion that would eventually rival his love of nature — he revelled in watching smartly uniformed troops marching with precision across the parade grounds. When the call to arms was sounded against the Fenian threat, Sam answered by enlisting in the 35th Regiment of the Simcoe Battalion of Infantry.

Sam saw no action against the Fenians, but he jumped at the opportunity to take officer training at Toronto, in which he excelled, and was commissioned as a junior officer. From the start, Sam seemed to instinctively grasp how the challenges ahead would demand more than physical stamina and raw courage — they would call for self-discipline and, above all, meticulous planning. Military training harnessed his energy and intelligence to strict habits of mind. Whatever his future ambitions, the orphaned lad from the woods of Ontario needed to make a living, so Sam bided his time as a clerk at Turnbull's Store while raising and training the Clarksburg Company of 31st Militia Regiment. By heredity, training, and spirit, Sam no doubt found the sedentary life of the shopkeeper restrictive, especially when the new Dominion of Canada was declared on July 1, 1867. He longed to be at the heart of the adventure that was this new country of Canada. Thanks to events that were to unfold far to the west, he would soon have the adventure he craved. There, in the Red River Settlement, Louis Riel was raising hell.

In the face of a threat of invasion from the U.S., military units were called to duty. Here the Governor General's Body Guard, a militia cavalry unit stationed in Toronto, poses for the formal unit photo (1866).

Taken in 1870 during the second Fenian Invasion, the Border Volunteers stand over a dead American Fenian.

The Famous Forty Red Sashes, named for the sashes they wore in battle, gather for a photo in 1870.

In 1938 the Steele home was still standing but was much the worse for wear.

TWO

The Red River Rebellion

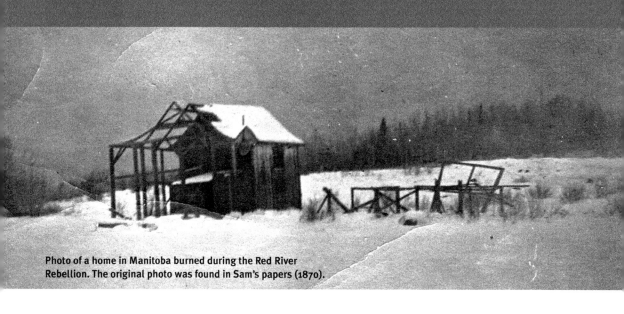

Photo of a home in Manitoba burned during the Red River
Rebellion. The original photo was found in Sam's papers (1870).

In the autumn of 1869 the Red River Settlement (soon to be the
province of Manitoba) was seething with rebellion. Under the terms
of Confederation, the territory was to be transferred from the ownership of the Hudson's Bay Company, Canada's oldest and largest trading
company, to the Dominion government in Ottawa.

For the most part, the Hudson's Bay Company had left the settlers
alone to figure out their affairs. For decades the farms in the area
had been laid out as long strips of land leading away from the rivers,
an arrangement that guaranteed a source of free, fresh water for
each family. With the transfer of power to Ottawa came government
surveyors who were ordered to lay out the farms in neat squares —
making them easy to administer, but cutting off many farms from a
water supply.

On October 10, 1869, Louis Riel and a band of other Métis used
threats of force to stop the surveyors. Appeals to Riel from Ottawa and
members of the community fell on deaf ears and battle lines were soon
drawn.

Riel quickly set up a provisional government and on November 24 took control of the Hudson's Bay Company's Fort Garry. By February 1870, Riel's force was five-hundred strong and making demands on the government in Ottawa. Donald Smith (later Lord Strathcona), Chief Officer of the Company, tried to persuade Riel and his men to lay down their arms.

An attempt to retake the fort was made by a group of citizens from Portage La Prairie, led by Major Charles Boulton, an ex-officer of the 100th Royal Canadian Regiment of the British Army. The group was captured, and one of the men, Thomas Scott, was executed after a show trial presided over by Riel. When word of Scott's killing reached Ottawa, it was quickly decided that force must be used to suppress the rebellion.

Colonel Garnet Wolseley, a British officer serving in Canada, was given command of the force tasked with capturing Riel. Wolseley quickly put out word for recruits and Sam Steele volunteered on May 1, 1870. Sam had been an officer with the 31st Grey Regiment, but he had resigned his commission. Assigned to No. 4 Company 1st Ontario Rifles, Sam was offered the chance to go to Manitoba as an officer, but he turned it down, believing that he needed to see a campaign as a regular soldier.

There was no good way to get from Ontario to Manitoba in 1870. The route chosen by the fighting force was an arduous one, with troops

Taken well after the Red River Rebellion ended, this photo shows a dog sled and the ruins of Upper Fort Garry, which had been captured by Louis Riel and others.

travelling by boat and foot more than 2,200 kilometres through the Canadian Shield. The force left Sault Ste. Marie, Ontario, on May 23 and landed in Thunder Bay on June 3. From there they embarked on canoes, accompanied by more than seven hundred voyageurs who were familiar with the territory. To avoid rapids and other dangers, the canoes were often portaged: beached, unloaded, and moved overland to the next safe waterway. The supplies were packed in bundles that weighed as much as forty kilograms each; carrying two of these over the uneven ground of the Canadian Shield was considered to be a feat of strength. Young Sam Steele was often seen carrying three and sometimes four of the bundles.

A contemporary drawing of Wolseley's camp as Sam and others prepared for the journey to Winnipeg, a trip that took ninety-four days.

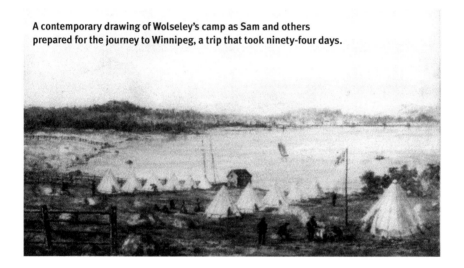

On August 27, Wolseley and his men landed at the Stone Fort (now Lower Fort Garry) — about twenty-four kilometres away from Riel's stronghold. In Sam's words:

> Early the next morning the force landed about two miles north of Winnipeg and advanced on Fort Garry, going round the west side of the village, but although guns were seen protruding from the embrasures in the bastions and the gate on the north side was shut, there were no signs of life, and the rebel flag had been hauled down. Scouts were sent round the fort at a gallop and found the south gate open; Riel and others were seen escaping over the bridge of boats in front of the fort. We then took possession of the place, hoisted the Union Jack, fired a salute and gave three cheers for the Queen.[1]

Wolseley's troops watched as Riel and his men slid across the border into the U.S. — without a shot being fired. However, Sam Steele knew he had found his calling.

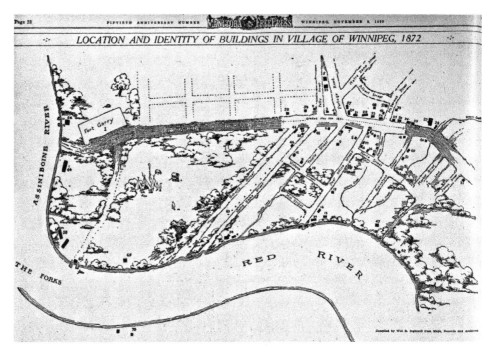

Sam stayed in Winnipeg for about a year after the end of the Red River Rebellion. Winnipeg was changing from a small village to a centre of commerce.

The north gate of Fort Garry today. It is all that is left of the once bustling fort in the heart of Winnipeg.

THREE

From Soldier to Mountie

This 1919 photo, taken from an aircraft, shows abandoned Fort Henry, where Sam served in the artillery.

Sam could have returned to Ontario immediately, but instead chose to stay in Manitoba. There was something about the wildness of the place that intrigued him. In the Canadian West, a man was judged by what he did, not who he was — a man could make a difference. For Sam it was a chance to learn more about soldiering and to sharpen his wilderness skills. But all good things must come to an end, and after a year Sam was ordered home.

On June 11, 1871, a train lumbered out of the Fort Garry station carrying Sam and a large contingent of soldiers back to Ontario, their duty in Manitoba done. Left behind to protect the new Province of Manitoba were one hundred men of the 2nd Quebec Rifles. When the men arrived in Toronto on July 14, many took their discharge and quietly drifted back to the farms and shops they had left more than a year earlier.

Sam knew he was destined to be a professional soldier in a country that preferred volunteer militias over a standing army. In the War of 1812 a small corps of professional soldiers, supported by Canadian volunteers and First Nations allies, turned back the much larger American invasion force. While the war ebbed and flowed over the next two years, the U.S. never achieved its objective of capturing the territory of Canada from the British. After the signing of the Treaty of Ghent brought the War of 1812 to an official close, the belief arose in Canada (supported by the British government) that the voluntary militias had won the war. For the next hundred years, Canada depended on citizen soldiers for its defence.

For a few months Sam served in Toronto in a response to a continuing, but diminishing, threat of Fenian invasion from the U.S. It was not the exciting life Sam craved, but it was soldiering. Then Sam's luck turned.

In October 1871, the Canadian government announced that it was forming a new battery of artillery and a school of gunnery — part of the new "Permanent Force." Within a few days Sam and his younger brother Richard were in Kingston, ready to take the year-long course.

Richard was the twenty-second man to sign up, Sam the twenty-third. The school was to be commanded by Lieutenant-Colonel George French of the Royal Artillery, a man who would take a major role in Sam's military career.

For the next two years Sam trained and then taught the militias in the area how to handle the cannon of the day. For Sam it was an idyllic time of military service and civilian parties around Kingston — he was rapidly becoming a trusted part of the Canadian military establishment.

However, in the West things were not so perfect. As American settlers pushed west, the Canadian government struggled to meet new challenges. American whiskey traders found a lucrative market among Aboriginal people both north and south of the 49th parallel — trading whiskey and guns for furs. The whiskey traders built trading posts that closely resembled armed forts, with little regard to the legal niceties of the international border. Without an armed force able to patrol the newly opened territories, Canada could do little to stop the trade — and the harm to the First Nations.

In 1873, Ottawa's hand was forced. A group of American wolf hunters had been trading relatively peacefully with the Assiniboine people in the Canadian Cypress Hills, about sixty-five kilometres north of the border. On June 1, a horse went missing from the wolfers' herd. Fuelled by alcohol, the Americans convinced themselves that someone from a nearby camp of Assiniboines must have stolen the horse. A decision was made to "clear out the camp." Under the cover of darkness, the Assiniboine camp was attacked; in minutes, twenty-three members of the band were dead and the hunters were racing for the protection of the border.

When word of the Cypress Hills Massacre reached Ottawa and was reported on by the press, Canadians demanded that the government of John A. Macdonald do something to protect Canada's territory and the Aboriginal people.

On a trip to Ottawa in August 1873, Sam learned that Macdonald was about to announce the activation of the North West Mounted Police (NWMP) and that the new force would be seeing action in the West. This was the life Sam craved. He would miss the camaraderie of garrison life in Kingston, but the chance to ride horses over the open prairies was a siren call. Through relatives, Sam arranged to meet the man then responsible for the new force — Major James Walsh.

Walsh told Sam he would be more than welcome in the NWMP — if he could obtain a release from the artillery battery back in Kingston. Sam raced back and asked Colonel French to allow him to join the NWMP and French quickly agreed. Little did Sam know that French had also signed up for the new force — as its first Commissioner.

FOUR

The Life of a Mountie

The legislation authorizing the establishment of the NWMP was introduced in May 1873; however, it took the Cypress Hills Massacre, which occured a week later, to force the frugal Macdonald government to come up with the funds required to actually make the new force a reality. The men were certainly not overpaid. At the same time the U.S. was spending $17 million on its army (more than the total budget of the entire Canadian government), pay for the new Canadian force was strictly enforced:

> Commissioner not exceeding $2000 a year and not less than $2,000; superintendent not exceeding $1,400 and not less than $1,000; paymaster not exceeding $1,000; quarter-master not exceeding $500; surgeon not exceeding $1,400 and not less than $1,000; veterinary surgeon not exceeding $600 and not less than $400; constable not exceeding $1.00 per day; sub-constable not exceeding 75c. per day.[2]

The mounted force was not to exceed more than three hundred men and, in addition to being a police force, its superintendents were to act as justices of the peace.

The newly appointed (now Inspector) James Walsh started recruiting in October 1873, looking for those of "... sound constitution,

In 1873 Sam was a handsome young officer when he decided to move to the new police force announced by the government of Sir John A. Macdonald.

active and able-bodied, able to ride, of good character, able to read and write either the English or French language, and between the ages of 18 and 40 years."[3] Sam met, or exceeded, the criteria on every count.

Sam soon found himself heading back to Manitoba and Lower Fort Garry. In an effort to keep costs down the first contingent consisted of only 150 men — a number Sam felt was "completely inadequate for the task."[4] It would become clear that more men were needed. In 1874, the Macdonald government would authorize another 150 men to be sent to Manitoba to bring the NWMP up to full strength of three hundred. Sam still felt the number too low, and commented that one thousand men would be needed to do the job, but the politicians in Ottawa thought otherwise.

The new force quickly took over Lower Fort Garry, the old Hudson's Bay Company Fort north of the village of Winnipeg. Sam recorded:

> Lt.-Col. [Lieutenant Colonel] Osborne Smith came down from Winnipeg and swore us in, each man being given a warrant with his name and rank, the first and last issued to the force. When my turn came Inspector Walsh said to the colonel, "I wish to recommend

In 1873 Sam was back in Manitoba serving at Lower Fort Garry, the new home of the NWMP just north of Winnipeg.

Sergeant-Major Steele to be confirmed in his rank," and Colonel Smith replied, "I am very glad, for my friend, Colonel French, who is commissioner, has requested me to appoint him.[5]

Sam was the third man officially sworn in.

Sam was soon in charge of both breaking semi-wild horses the NWMP had obtained in Manitoba and training men in the finer arts of riding. He demanded the men train five times a day — with classes lasting from six o'clock a.m. to sundown. All lessons were outside and were suspended only if the temperature dropped below -37 degrees Celsius. Many of the men had lied on their recruiting forms when it came to their riding abilities. Man after man fell off his horse, time and time again. The men complained of saddle sores caused by the constant training. Sam ordered the men be issued salt; rubbing it into their wounds formed saddle-tough callouses. One recruit reported, "We became so tough I could sit on a prickly pear."

It was not all hard work. Lower Fort Garry was often the site of dinners and balls — all of which served to distract the officers and men and to raise morale. Sam would later write in his autobiography:

Winter was harsh at Lower Fort Garry — in 1873 and today.

There was a Quadrille Club for the N.C.O.'s and men, but I never attended, as I much preferred an evening either with the old settlers, who could tell me something about the country, or in attending their dances and weddings. I took notes of all the information I received, and was pretty well acquainted with the customs of the Indians, hunters and traders before I left Fort Garry.[6]

Sam had anticipated, and was prepared for, the order to march west.

FIVE

The Great March West

A famous contemporary print shows the new men of the NWMP encountering buffalo for the first time. The giant animals provided food and other necessities as the force moved west (1873).

S am's newfound knowledge of the West was about to come in very handy indeed.

On June 7, 1874, the entire Mounted police force left Lower Fort Garry, heading to Dufferin, Manitoba — about sixteen kilometres north of the Manitoba-U.S. border. There Sam and the others waited for more men to arrive by train from Toronto before turning to the West. The Great March West was about to begin.

Colonel French reported:

> To a stranger it would have appeared an astonishing cavalcade, armed men and guns looked as if fighting was to be done. What could ploughs, harrows, mowing machines, cows, calves, etc., be for? But that little force had a double duty to perform, to fight if necessary, but in any case to establish posts in the far west.[7]

The whole expedition almost ended before it started when a massive thunderstorm hit the NWMP camp, stampeding the horses. Men spent days gathering up the horses from as much as eighty kilometres away — only sheer exhaustion stopped the horses in their mad dash.

On June 8, the NWMP left camp, but travelled only sixteen kilometres that first day. Sam referred to it as a "Hudson's Bay Start." A short first day allowed everyone a chance to test out horses, draft teams, saddles, and other equipment.

The next day the column of men, horses, and cattle pushed west. At first the march went well. The land and weather of southern Manitoba allowed for relatively rapid travel parallel to the U.S. border. By July 29, they had reached Short Creek, on the banks of the Souris by La Roche Percée. From there the column split in two, with Inspector William Jarvis (a senior officer), along with Sam, taking the sick and injured 1,400 kilometres northwest to Fort Edmonton as the rest of the force continued west. Sam described the Edmonton-bound group as the "quartermaster and several of the youngest and weakest men, 55 sick and almost played-out horses recovering from a severe attack of epizo- otic, 24 waggons, 55 ox-carts with 12 drivers, 62 oxen, 50 cows and 50 calves." The challenge had just begun.

For the next eight weeks Sam and the others struggled with a lack of food for the horses, wretched weather, poor or non-existent roads, and illness among the men. Sam described the trek as the worst he had ever undergone. According to Sam the trail "… was knee-deep in black mud, sloughs crossed it every few hundred yards, and the wagons had

As the NWMP prepared for the "Great March West," a storm hit their camp at Dufferin, Manitoba, in the summer of 1873. Horses stampeded and Sam and other officers spent days rounding up the last of the strays.

to be unloaded and dragged through them by hand."[8] He went on to describe the trek as the worst he had ever undergone:

> Many small ponds covered with a thin coating of ice lined the sides of the trail, and gave us much trouble while we were engaged in unloading the waggons. The poor animals, crazed with thirst and feverish because of their privations, would rush to the ponds to drink, often falling and having to be dragged out with ropes from where they fell. One of the men would hold up their heads while I placed the hitch. It mattered not how

often they were watered, the same performance had to
be gone through time after time.[9]

Sam was modest. Men reported that he often grabbed the horns of a cow
caught in the mud and, using his brute strength, wrestled the beast free.

Jarvis and Sam finally arrived at Fort Edmonton on August 3, 1874,
having travelled more than 2,500 kilometres, the longest recorded expedition carrying its own supplies. Jarvis formally reported that Steele had
done the "manual labour of at least two men" on the journey.

SIX

Treaties with the First Nations

When the NWMP first encountered the First Nations people, neither was sure what to expect of the other. Over time respect grew between the two groups (1877).

S am's official reports often included words like "squaw" and "Redskin" when discussing Aboriginal people. It was the language of the day, but was not an indicator of disrespect for the First Nations peoples. In fact, Sam recognized his own passions in their way of life, and highly respected them as hunters, warriors, and individuals, a respect that was often returned. Sam described Métis leader Gabriel Dumont as someone whose "good qualities far outweighed his bad, and he was a man whom many leading white men were glad to call friend. One might travel the plains from one end to the other and talk to the Métis hunters and never hear an unkind word said of Dumont."[10]

Sam's attitude toward Aboriginal people was not unusual in the Canadian West. Many settlers from Eastern Canada — be they policemen, ranchers, or farmers — saw them as neighbours and fellow survivors in what could often be a harsh land. The very founding of the NWMP was based on protecting them from American whiskey traders and wolf hunters; south of the border, law enforcement often had as its goal the subjugation of the First Nations. Many Aboriginal people worked directly for the NWMP as hunters, guides, and trackers. For the members of the NWMP, they were colleagues, and those who did not see it that way did not last long on the frontier.

The new police force stayed true to its military roots; parades and drill made up much of an officer's day (1877).

The First Nations also respected the NWMP, on the whole. While they did not always agree with the decisions of the policemen — who were also the judges — they accepted that the NWMP were usually fair in their dealings. Queen Victoria was referred to as the Great White Mother and the NWMP were acknowledged as her representatives.

Sam spent a great deal of time studying Aboriginal people, their customs, and their traditions. He knew where and when they hunted; he watched as they celebrated special occasions. Sam worked to build better relations with his prairie neighbours. His writings to friends and family often complained that it would take very little to win over the First Nations, but that, out of ignorance, Ottawa often set policies that adversely affected Aboriginal people.

Throughout 1876 the government in Ottawa negotiated Treaty 7 with the Plains Indians. This treaty (along with Treaties 1 through 6) would see the First Nations cede their rights to the vast western prairies in exchange for land (reserves), education, health care, protection from American whiskey traders, and cash payments (usually on a yearly basis.)

On August 6, 1877, Sam received orders to immediately take the NWMP headquarters staff based in Swan River, Manitoba, and most of D Division to Fort Carlton for the signing of Treaty 6. Within three hours, the men had departed, and they arrived at Fort Carlton, 1,850 kilometres away, on August 18.

The NWMP contingent arrived just as the first day's events were drawing to a close. Present from the government were the Honourable Alexander Morris, lieutenant governor of Manitoba and the North West Territories, the Honourable W.J. Christie, a former Chief Factor of the Hudson Bay Company, and the Honourable James Mackay, also formally employed by the Hudson's Bay Company; both fluent in the languages of the First Nations. Treaty 6 was signed on September 9, 1877.

Sam immediately headed for Blackfoot Crossing, near Calgary. More than four thousand Aboriginal people, representing the Siksika, Kainai, Piikani, Tsuu Tina, and Stoney, were present for the negotiating and signing of Treaty 7.

After some days of deliberation, on September 28, 1877, the chiefs who were present all agreed to sign the treaty.

Chief Crowfoot spoke at the signing:

> The plains are large and wide; we are the children of the plains; it has been our home and the buffalo have been our food always. I hope you look upon the Blackfeet, Bloods, Peigans and Sarcees as your children now, and that you will be indulgent and charitable to them. The advice given to me and my people has proved to be very good. If the police had not come to this country, where should we all be now? Bad men and whiskey were indeed killing us so fast that very few of us indeed would have been left today. The Mounted Police have protected us as the feathers of the bird protect it from the frosts of winter … I am satisfied. I will sign the treaty.[11]

The treaties were the beginning of a long relationship between First Nations peoples, the NWMP, and Sam Steele.

Chief Sitting Bull (1877).

An old photo postcard entitled "After an Indian Battle" was almost certainly a staged photo to be sold in Eastern Canada.

A Blood Nation traditional form of burial on the prairies.

Sam's reputation was growing throughout the new country of Canada, as well as across the border in the United States. In the same year he attended the signing of the treaties, Sam was asked to negotiate with famous Aboriginal leader Sitting Bull.

After the crushing defeat of General George Custer and his fighting force at Little Bighorn, Sitting Bull moved his people north to Canada to avoid American retribution. Sam joined U.S. Army General Alfred Howe Terry to meet with Sitting Bull. While they failed to convince Sitting Bull to return to the U.S., Sam and Inspector James Walsh developed a close relationship with the American chief that lasted until the Sioux returned south of the border four years later.

SEVEN

Rail Strike

The end of the rail line moved every day as the CPR
snaked its way across the prairies.

As the rail line moved west, few could resist the chance for a photo with the giant, and noisy, locomotives.

I n February 1882, while on personal leave in Ottawa, Sam was summoned to the office of Prime Minister John A. Macdonald. Macdonald wanted Sam to take personal charge of policing the building of the new railway that was snaking its way from eastern Canada to British Columbia. The new westernmost province had entered Confederation on the promise of a rail link through the mountains and back to lucrative markets in Quebec and Ontario. The Canadian Pacific Railway (CPR) was to keep that promise.

When another officer had fallen ill, Sam had taken over his job of recruiting an extra two hundred men for the NWMP. Sam quickly found someone to take his place as recruiter and returned to Fort Qu'appelle, in what would become the province of Saskatchewan. He was appointed acting adjutant of the region and placed in command of the NWMP detachments on the new CPR line.

Construction camps along the rail line were full of tough men, sometimes paid, sometimes unpaid for weeks. Sam and his men found the camps a real change from regular police work.

Camp cars followed the rail lines into the mountains providing food and sometimes shelter to the "navvies" working on the line.

Sam followed the construction of the CPR, moving whenever the rail crews did. In addition to his regular policing duties, he was often pressed into dealing with labour strikes, such as the one at Maple Creek in the spring of 1883. He found a way to end the labour strike peacefully and quickly became a favourite of both the company and the labourers. Both groups recognized that Sam could always be counted on to act in a fair and balanced matter, no matter how trying the circumstances.

February and March 1885 found Sam again at the railhead, which was now at Beaver, B.C., well into the mountain passes of the Rockies. The management of the CPR was constantly short of money and often did not pay the men on the work crews (known as navvies) who were doing the heavy labour of laying track and digging tunnels. With the company three months behind in paying the workers, open revolt was in the air. Sam had tried to warn both the prime minister and company officials that serious trouble was brewing and that a riot was a very real possibility. His messages went unheeded.

The workers threw down their tools and struck on April 1, 1885. It couldn't have come at a worse time for Sam, who had come down with a serious fever and had been ordered to his bed by a doctor.

Not all of the workers agreed with the strike. Those who tried to return to their jobs were being intimidated by more than three hundred

In one of the most famous pictures in Canadian history, Lord Strathcona, in the white beard, drives the last spike completing the building of the CPR line across Canada. In the background, peering over the crowd, is a moustached Sam Steele.

Sam and his men pose for an informal picture. With the photography technology of the day the pose would have been held for a full minute or more.

strikers — some armed with pistols and shotguns. When word reached Sam that violence was imminent, he ordered that his eight men were to use everything at their disposal to ensure work continued on the rail line.

On April 2, Sam's men did assist the workers to return to the rail-head, but only after they had been fired on and threatened by the strikers. When one of the strikers was arrested, his friends threatened to take him from jail — using force if necessary. The situation had become completely unacceptable.

Sam struggled out of his sickbed. Barely able to walk, he picked up a Winchester rifle and, backed only by his eight Mounties, headed toward the crowd of two hundred angry workers.

A work crew poses for the camera, demonstrating laying tracks along the CPR line. In reality the scene would have been much more hectic with hundreds of men racing to get their work done.

When it was built, the Stoney Creek Bridge was the highest in the world.

Supported by his men and a number of citizens who were on the side of law and order, Sam ordered the strikers to "Listen to this, and keep your hands off your guns, or I will shoot the first man of you who makes a hostile movement." He went on:

> Johnston then read the Riot Act, and when he had finished I said, "You have taken advantage of the fact that a rebellion has broken out in the northwest and that I have only a handful of men, but, as desperate diseases require desperate remedies, and both disease and remedy are here, I warn you that if I find more than twelve of you standing together or any large crowd assembled I will open fire upon you and mow you down. Now disperse at once and behave yourselves.[12]

The strikers were not happy but, facing Sam's resolve and the other armed officers, they gave up and returned to their tents and cabins. Troubles had been avoided and work on the railway continued.

Sam finished his association with the CPR on November 7, 1885, when he was personally invited to join James Ross, Manager of Construction, and W.C. Van Horne, Manager of the CPR, as they witnessed Donald Smith (later Lord Strathcona) drive the last spike at Craigelaichie, B.C. The trans-Canada railroad was completed.

At the summit of the Rogers Pass, the highest point on the line, a small town sprung up to serve the men on the work crews.

Glacier House was a hotel built along the CPR line to serve the thousands of tourists and business travellers that could now travel, by train, from the east coast to the west.

EIGHT

Policing the West

For the NWMP the first shelter in the West was provided by military
bell tents as forts and more permanent structures were built (1877).

In 1877, Fort MacLeod, in what is now southern, modern-day Alberta, was little more than shacks and mud roads.

S am spent a total of fifteen years moving from post to post throughout the Canadian West. In 1882, while still policing the CPR, he was tasked with developing a new headquarters of the NWMP in the West. The site he chose was located near a small railway stop known as "Pile of Bones." Today, this site houses the Royal Canadian Mounted Police Training Depot at Regina, Saskatchewan.

In 1888, Superintendent Sam Steele was made commanding officer of Fort MacLeod. While in this position, he described his routine:

> I had not a moment to spare. In addition to the endless routine, a party under my supervision was employed broncho busting. The remainder of the force was kept busy at the barrack routine of a cavalry regiment, guarding prisoners, heading off whisky traders and horse-thieves, visiting Indian camps and traders' posts. The court-room was crowded nearly every day; the assistant commissioner and Inspector Winder were frequently on the bench and, in addition to my numerous outdoor duties, I attended court regularly, producing witnesses and preparing all details. Scarcely a night passed without an excursion after some criminal cases, and our men were continuously on the trail of law-breakers.[13]

Sam and other NWMP members often patrolled the vast prairies alone. There were just not enough men to provide two-man patrols. The solo patrols continued even when the temperature dropped as low as -50 degrees Celsius in winter. Often the police depended on the kindness of farmers and ranchers in the region to provide food and shelter.

Contrary to the peaceful settlement of the Canadian west often portrayed in history books, crime was rampant and many people carried

Calgary, two hundred kilometres north of Fort MacLeod, offered a few more amenities in 1878, but life was still hard.

In the Cypress Hills, Fort Walsh was an important location from which to control the illegal liquor trade originating south of the Canada-U.S. border (1878).

Sam, without the hat, sits among his officers at Fort Walsh in 1879.

firearms — for hunting and for self-defence. A number of NWMP officers were killed while executing their duties.

The senior officers of the NWMP were in a unique legal position. In addition to being policemen, they were also magistrates. It was their job to rule on the evidence provided to them by the men they commanded. Such power in the hands of law enforcement would be seen as intolerable today, but in the 1880s in western Canada, Sam and others made the system work.

The NWMP were very much a part of community life in western Canada. For MacLeod was often a scene of social parties and other events. Sam described one Christmas celebration at the fort:

> Our Christmas dinners in the Mounted Police were always in the evenings, no daylight dinners for us. All, from the commissioner to the latest recruit, realized that Christmas comes but once a year, and that we must have a good time. Our civilian friends, to the number of 20, sat down with us, and our bill of fare consisted of turkeys, wild geese, antelope, other venison, buffalo tongues, boss

On January 15, 1890, Sam Steele and Marie Elizabeth de Lotbiniere Harwood were married in Vaudreuil, Quebec. The couple met when Marie was visiting her aunt, the wife of a NWMP officer. Sam was committed to Marie until the day he died.

rib, plum pudding, California fruit, raisins, nuts and milk punch, for which a permit had been obtained to enable us to pass the Christmas satisfactorily.

The NWMP community included members of the First Nations. Many of the plains hunters came to towns such as Fort MacLeod to trade buffalo hides and other furs they had collected. Sam ensured there was always a strong NWMP presence on trading days to guarantee that Aboriginal traders were not cheated. He wrote:

> We had by this time become very well acquainted with the Indians and had a very great influence over them. They were learning to shun the low white man and look to us for protection. … The Indians had a name for every white man they knew…. Colonel Macleod was a great favourite with them, and the fort was called "The place where the 'Bull's Head' stays." He was regarded by the Blackfeet Nation as the personification of justice. I doubt if anyone ever had such influence with them.[14]

Sam Steele in his finest NWMP uniform, circa 1892.

Sam's personal diary for 1892. Like all Victorian military officers, Sam kept a daily diary and only stopped making entries a few days before his death.

DAILY JOURNAL
1892

N. W. M. P.

Timeline for Sam Steele
Policing the West:

Spring 1875	Sam Steele, after planning and building a new headquarters, moves with his men to Fort Saskatchewan.
August 1875	Sam receives a promotion to Chief Constable and is transferred to the NWMP headquarters at Swan River Barracks located in Livingstone, Saskatchewan.
Summer 1876	Sam is put in charge of moving the headquarters to Fort MacLeod.
July 26, 1878	Sam is promoted to sub-inspector, moving to Fort Walsh in the Cypress Hills.
1880	Sam is now an inspector and commands B Division at Fort Qu'Appelle, Saskatchewan — his first independent command.
February 1882	Sam, temporarily stationed in Winnipeg, is in charge of recruiting two hundred new members for the NWMP.

Summer 1882	Sam officially takes over the CPR construction zone. Sam polices liquor sales, gambling, and prostitution among the four thousand railroad workers.
Summer 1882	Sam establishes the NWMP post at Pile of Bones — modern Regina. The RCMP training depot is still active in Regina.
1883	Sam is placed in command of Fort Calgary.
April 1884	Steele is appointed a Federal Commissioner by Sir John A Macdonald and follows the rail line into B.C.
1885	Sam leads Steele's Scouts in the Riel Rebellion against Louis Riel and Gabriel Dumont.
August 1885	Sam is promoted to Superintendent.
November 7, 1885	Sam attends the driving of the Last Spike at Craigellachie in Eagle Pass. He then rides the first train to make the journey to the Pacific coast.
1886	Sam serves at Fort MacLeod in southern Alberta.
June 1887	Sam and seventy-five men are sent to the interior of BC where they build a post later known as Fort Steele.
August 9, 1888	Sam and his men return to Lethbridge, Alberta, via the Crowsnest Pass.
December 8, 1888	Sam is promoted to the command of Fort MacLeod.

On December 7, 1891, Sam and Marie welcomed their new daughter, Mary Charlotte Flora Macdonald Steele, to the world. Sam loved all of his children but Flora would always be his favourite (1895).

The Steeles' second daughter, Gertrude Alexandra Elizabeth Steele, was born on August 2, 1895 (1897).

NINE

Riel Rebellion

During the Riel Rebellion, the new NWMP headquarters Sam had established at Regina was the centre of preparation for military activities in the West (1885).

I n the spring of 1885 Sam once again met Louis Riel during a rebellion. This time, however, there was no peaceful end to the campaign.

In January 1885 Sam was receiving reports from various NWMP detachments that all was quiet in the West. By March that had all changed. Various detachments were reporting that the Métis people in the North West Territories, an area then comprising modern Saskatchewan and Alberta, were restless and talking about revolt. They wrote, "Half-breed rebellion liable to break out at any moment. Troops must be largely reinforced. If half-breeds rise the Indians will join them." (Throughout official documents of the time the Métis were described as half-breeds, a term used, and accepted, in the 1880s.)

The Métis were agitating about land reforms ordered from Ottawa, as they had in 1870, and the Cree were frustrated with the lack of action on many of the prmises in Treaty 7. Food had been slow in coming and some of the Indian agents were taking advantage of Aboriginal people. To the Métis and First Nations, violence seemed to be to only option. Gabriel Dumont, the son of a French-Canadian father and an Aboriginal mother, was well-known as a Métis leader in the region. Dumont had a reputation as being fair but tough, someone who would defend Métis rights against both the First Nations and the Government of Canada as adjutant-general and commander of forces in the provisional Métis government.

On March 26, 1885, a group of Métis led by Dumont tried to steal supplies from a store at Duck Lake, in what is now central Saskatchewan. The occupants of the store Dumont and the others were robbing resisted, shots were fired, and the NWMP responded by sending more men to the area. When the Mounties were attacked by the rebels, it was clear that war could not be avoided. To make matters worse, Dumont had brought Louis Riel back to Canada to lead the rebellion along with him.

A group of "irregulars" (volunteers who brought their own horses and equipment to the fight) pose with a NWMP member (1885).

A troop of NWMP, with a row of wagons in the background, prepares to move out in support of the Canadian government's efforts to quell the rebellion in Saskatchewan (1885).

Ottawa's response was to order British General Frederick Dobson Middleton (who was serving in Canada) and 1,300 men to put down the rebellion. Coming from Eastern Canada, it took the force some time to arrive, and until it did the NWMP were responsible for defending towns and remote outposts.

Sam arrived at Calgary on April 11, and was quickly recruited by retired General Thomas Bland Strange, who had been tasked to take a force north through what would become Alberta and attack the Métis and Cree from the west. Strange asked Sam to take over scouting duties and promoted Sam to Major and Commander of the Cavalry and Scouts of the Alberta Field Force. His force, officially known as

Steele's Scouts, was made up of ranchers and NWMP officers. Sam was back in the army.

Steele's Scouts were responsible for chasing down and arresting Cree war chief Big Bear. The Scouts, hearing that Big Bear and his band had killed a number of people at Frog Lake, Alberta, headed to Edmonton on April 20. Following the North Saskatchewan River, Sam and his men chased the fleeing Aboriginal band. They finally ran the First Nations force to ground in July 1885. This conflict stands as the last armed battle on Canadian soil.

Major General Strange wrote of Sam, "Major Steele and his cavalry were the eyes, ears and feelers of the force, and their spirited pursuit of

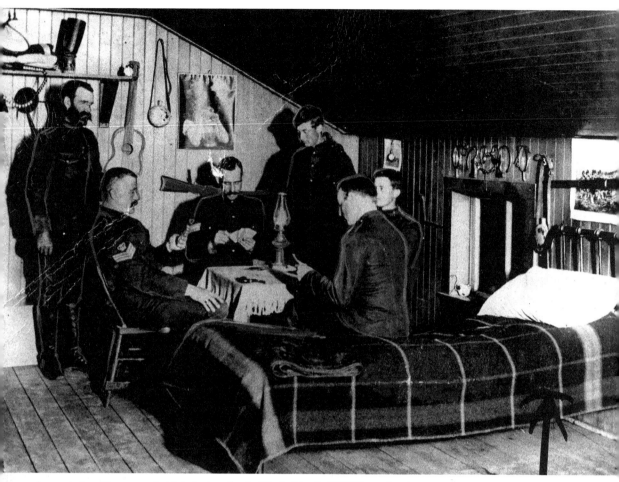

A rare photo, with some period "photoshopping," of the inside of a NWMP barracks, circa 1885.

Big Bear crowned with success the long and weary march which they had protected and, to a certain extent, guided."

Despite his superior's accolades, Sam always believed that the rebellion itself could have been avoided. Knowing the Métis and Cree of the region, he felt that their demands were reasonable and would not have cost Ottawa a great deal to address. Instead, a war was fought and Sam witnessed some of the goodwill between the NWMP and the First Nations be lost forever.

By 1885 Fort MacLeod had become a major NWMP staging
post and photographers were there to capture the moment.

TEN

Keeping the Peace

The barracks at Fort Steele in the
Canadian Kootenays, circa 1887.

After the Riel Rebellion, Sam returned to the NWMP as a
Superintendent — his former rank. One of the few officers to
find his reputation enhanced after the Riel Rebellion, Sam soon
found himself sent to avert another First Nations uprising — this time
further west.

Sam was serving in Lethbridge, near the U.S.-Alberta border on
May 20, 1887, when he received orders to take a group of men to
the Kootenay district of central British Columbia. According to Sam's
autobiography:

> The duty for which we were detailed was to restore
> order amongst the Indians of the Kootenay district,

Looking into the barracks square, Fort Steele (1887).

then almost inaccessible, there being no way in during
the winter, except on snowshoes, and during the
summer only by pack trail. The settlers in the district
were very few in number and uneasy on account of
Chief Isadore, of the Kootenay tribe, having, with part
of his band, broken open the gaol at Wild Horse Creek,
an old mining camp, and released Kapula, one of their
men who had been arrested, charged with the murder,
in 1884, of two white placer miners at Deadman's
Creek on the Wild Horse-Golden trail. Isadore then
ordered Provincial Constable Anderson, who had made
the arrest, and the Hon. F. Aylmer out of the district,
forbidding them to return.[15]

On July 30, 1887, Sam arrived at Six Mile Creek — a spot that had
been recommended to him for the location of a fort by locals. Sam
found the area completely unacceptable and wrote to the Commissioner
of the NWMP for permission to move to a new location, which was
quickly given.

Sam immediately moved his men to a spot that "commanded
the trails to Tobacco Plains, the Crow's Nest Pass, Moyea, and the
Columbia Lakes, and was the most central situation from which to
communicate with the Indians and give protection to the whites."

Crews lay out the new fort that Sam had been ordered to build. Little
did he know it would be named after him on its completion (1887).

The stable at Fort Steele. There was little difference between where the men stayed and where the horses stayed (1887).

His first task was to get his men building the new fort. Then he called for Chief Isadore to come to the NWMP camp. Sam spoke at length about the role the new fort would take in the life of the Kootenays and how Isadore and his people had to respect the authority of the government in Ottawa. Isadore informed Sam that a number of Chinese and white people in the area had told him that the NWMP meant to harm the First Nations people. Sam quickly recognized that criminals in the area were trying to drive a wedge between the NWMP and Isadore.

Sam responded that "[the NWMP] were in the district to maintain the laws of the Great Mother, and that both whites and Indians would receive just treatment and would be equally severely punished if they deserved it."[16]

Sam was able to report that there were very few cases of lawlessness among the Aboriginal people in the year that followed, and that reforms in allotting land had delivered the desired effect of quelling any rebellion in the region.

This time, Sam's personal strength and sense of justice won over a First Nations people and brought peace to what only a few years before had been a volatile region. When Sam returned to Fort MacLeod, he left behind a post that in 1888 had been renamed Fort Steele by the grateful citizens in the area.

Troop Quarters, Fort Steele (1887).

Another view of the Troop Quarters at Fort Steele (1887).

ELEVEN

Yukon Gold Rush

Canadian officers stand on the boundary line separating Alaska and the Yukon. With the discovery of gold it was one of the most popular, and foreboding, crossing points between the two countries (1898).

If there is anything in the world that can bring out the worst in men, it is gold fever. In August 1896, gold was found in Bonanza Creek in the Yukon Territory. Word quickly spread up and down the Yukon River Valley. Miners staked out Bonanza, Eldorado, and Hunker Creeks in the hope of striking it rich.

In July 1897, word reached the United States that gold had been discovered in the Canadian North, and the rush began in earnest.

Men, many suffering from the effects of a recession at home, headed to California and Oregon to board boats headed for Skagway and Dyea, Alaska.

Most of the prospective miners were not used to the wilderness life. They were teachers, doctors, lawyers, and other professionals. Ahead of them was a gruelling trip just to get to the gold fields. They had to travel, on foot, forty kilometres along the Chilkoot Trail and then over the 1,000-metre-high Chilkoot Pass or the 880-metre-high White Pass to the Yukon River. From there they built rafts and headed down the turbulent Yukon River to Dawson in the Yukon Territory — 800 kilometres away. Many would try to cross the passes without enough food or equipment, believing that they would simply buy the supplies they needed in Dawson when they found gold. For many, this would mean death from starvation or exposure.

The final straw for the Canadian government came when armed criminals from Skagway were reported to be setting up in Dawson. While there had been a NWMP presence in the territory since 1894, it was determined that the nineteen-man force was nowhere near up to the job. Their commanding officer, Inspector Charles Constantine, was himself a justice of the peace, land agent, customs officer, postmaster, and Indian agent, in addition to registering all mines in the territory and attending to his policing duties.

There would have to be a larger NWMP presence in the North — and soon.

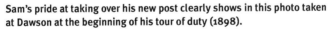

Sam's pride at taking over his new post clearly shows in this photo taken at Dawson at the beginning of his tour of duty (1898).

Dawson City was a busy place when Sam first landed there. Paddlewheelers were so common there was often not enough room for all of them to dock at the same time (1898).

A typical NWMP post in the Yukon during the gold rush (1898).

In another classic Canadian photo, would-be gold miners head over the Chilkoot Pass and into the gold fields on the Canadian side (1899).

Heggs & Co.
PHOTOS,
DAWSON.

Sam, in his field uniform complete with sword, poses for a photo sitting on a chair made from moose antlers (1900).

On January 29, 1898, Sam was once again ordered to pack up and leave, this time for the Yukon. Leaving his wife and three children in Fort MacLeod for Vancouver, on February 6 he boarded the *Thistle* heading for Skagway, Alaska. More than two hundred men were wedged aboard the thirty-six-metre-long Alaskan sealing boat for the 1,770-kilometre voyage. Sam described the weather as "very severe; snowstorms and hurricanes raged, and the seas, as we crossed Queen Charlotte Sound and Dixon Entrance, tossed our little craft as if it were a cockleshell."

When the *Thistle* finally landed at Skagway on February 14, 1898, the town of five thousand was suffering under -30-degree temperatures and hurricane-force winds. Sam found a room at the local hotel and then reported to the NWMP office in the American town. He was ready to take on his new command.

Early on the morning of February 21, 1898, Sam left for the Chilkoot Pass. The weather was so bitter he was forced to spend the night at a stable that had been built halfway up the steep incline.

Sam was amazed at the conditions he found at the top of the passes. In his autobiography, he describes the conditions faced by Inspector Belcher (an old friend) and his men:

> The camp on the Chilkoot ... was pitched on the summit, where it is bounded by high mountains. A wooden cabin was erected in a couple of days; the place where it was in the pass was only about 100 yards [91 metres] wide.... The nearest firewood was 7 miles [11 kilometres] away, and the man sent for it often returned badly frost-bitten. Belcher, collecting customs, performing military as well as police duty on the summits, lived in the shack, which had all the discomforts of a shower bath. Snow fell so thickly and constantly that everything was damp and papers became mildewed. From February 25 to March 3 the weather was dry and cold, but on that date another terrific storm began and continued almost uninterrupted until May 1! This storm reached its height on Saturday, the 3rd, when the snow buried the cabin and all the tents on the summit, the snowfall for the day being 6 feet [1.8 metres] on the level.[17]

Establishing himself at the head of the Lynn Canal, Sam quickly set to work managing the main entrance to the gold fields. He had a

Sports day in Dawson on July 4, 1899.

1901 Whitehorse. At Whitehorse the paddlewheelers brought a constant stream of miners
and the supplies necessary to survive in the harsh weather of the Canadian North (1901).

Main Street, Dawson City, circa 1899.

reputation for prodigious work, starting as early as 4:00 a.m. each day and working until midnight.

By November 1895, Sam was commanding a force of 285 officers and men. The NWMP continued to be the embodiment of the law in the North. The Mounties also ensured that each man who crossed the Chilkoot and White Passes had a year's worth of supplies with him, that boats and rafts met safety standards, and that only experienced pilots were navigating the frail boats through the most difficult sections of the Yukon River.

Sam wrote that "the whole demeanour of the people changed the moment they crossed the summit. The pistol was packed in the valise and not used. The desperado, if there, had changed his ways. No one feared him."

Some newcomers to the area did break the law; Sam often sentenced them to chop wood for the use of the NWMP garrison.

On September 26, 1899, Sam's time in the North finished. He had received instructions to head to Ottawa where new orders awaited him. On the way, he stopped in Montreal to reunite with his wife and children, who had moved to the city to be closer to Marie's relatives. It was the first time they had seen each other in almost eighteen months. The reunion was to be a short one, however — Sam was destined to head for South Africa and the war brewing there.

A group of miners pose for a photo with their dog. For many of them the photo would be the only keepsake from their time in the Yukon. Some struck it rich but many more never found any gold at all (1898).

TWELVE

The Boer War

Strathcona's Horse, the newly formed regiment paid for by Lord Strathcona, lines up for its first ever photograph. In a matter of weeks the snow would be left behind for the rolling hills of South Africa.

While Sam had been bringing law and order to the Canadian North, England and the empire had gone to war in South Africa.

The Boers, white settlers of Dutch ancestry, had inhabited portions of South Africa for almost a hundred years when the Second Boer War broke out in 1899. The Boers, centred predominantly in the Transvaal Republic and the Orange Free State, felt threatened by the continual expansion of the British government in other areas of South Africa.

Sam, the first colonel of the Strathcona's, poses with the King's Colours.

Sam and his daughter Flora just before he left for South Africa.

With the discovery of diamonds in 1871 at Kimberly and the discovery of gold in the Transvaal in 1886, the die was cast. As more and more British citizens and other foreigners moved to the Transvaal and Orange Free State to work in the gold mines, the resentment of the original settlers built. The Boers started to push back. Occasionally, these encounters turned violent, and the British government felt it had to step in to protect its citizens.

The British and Boer governments entered a long phase of negotiations, focusing on the rights of the foreigners within the Boer States (including the right to vote), the rights of the non-white population, control of the mining industry, and the future of the two Boer states (Britain wanted to bring them into the British Empire). When negotiations collapsed in September 1899, the British demanded full rights for all British citizens in the Boer states. The Boers, in turn, demanded that all British citizens leave the Transvaal and Orange Free States. When Britain refused the Boer demands, the Boers declared war.

At first, Britain felt that her superior army and navy would bring the war to a quick and victorious end. But the Boers quickly struck the British territories of Natal and Cape Colony and besieged the British garrisons of Ladysmith, Mafeking, and Kimberly. To add insult to injury, when Britain tried to break the sieges, the Boers scored victories and drove the British back.

When it became clear that the war was going to go on longer than expected, Britain asked for help from the Empire — including Canada.

English-speaking Canada and the Conservative party were almost universally in support of sending troops in support of the British war effort. The governing Liberal party was more hesitant. Much of its support came from French Canadians, who were adamantly opposed to the war. Finally, after much debate, Prime Minister Wilfrid Laurier agreed to send a thousand soldiers of the Royal Canadian Regiment to South Africa.

Wealthy men like Donald Smith, Lord Strathcona, a former clerk in the Hudson's Bay Company who had risen to great power, privately contacted the government to ask what they could do to help. The result was that Lord Strathcona committed more than $1 million (about $30 million today) of his own money to establish, equip, train, and transport to South Africa a new cavalry unit. Lord Strathcona wanted to make his donation anonymously but, when word of his generosity leaked out, the prime minister would insist the new force bear Strathcona's name. Once the first Canadian contingent was well on its way to South Africa, the Canadian government turned its attention to what its next response should be. When Sam heard rumours that a NWMP contingent was being recruited to fight the Boers, he quickly volunteered. He was offered the second-in-command position in what would be a composite regiment of permanent cavalry made up of NWMP officers and cowboys (not unlike the Steele's Scouts force Sam commanded in 1885). Sam hesitated and finally turned down the command. It was clear that he had not come this far to be second to anybody.

Sam was contacted by Frederick Borden, the Minister of Militia, and ordered to Ottawa; Sam was to command the regiment that Lord Strathcona had donated to the Canadian government. He was again to lead a group of mounted riflemen into battle, alongside officers from the NWMP who had volunteered. Sam immediately started recruiting and equipping the new force. By February 8, 1900, all was in place, and men and horses were on the way to Ottawa. They arrived at Landsdowne Park Exhibition Grounds in Ottawa on February 14.

A party of well wishers lines the docks as the Strathcona's board the SS *Monterey* for the long voyage to South Africa (1900).

The Strathcona's camp at Cape Town, South Africa (1900).

After the usual round of dinners and parades, the newly named Lord Strathcona's Horse were ready for the journey to South Africa, and boarded the SS *Monterey* at Halifax on March 17. All together, Sam's command included twenty-eight officers, 512 men, and 599 horses.

Three weeks from Canada, the *Monterey* anchored in Table Bay, South Africa.

After spending time acclimatizing to the weather and the British way of running an army, Sam and his men were ordered once again to board ships. They were to head north along the coast to Kosi Bay and destroy vital railway bridges, to stop the Boers from getting supplies. When British Intelligence reported that the Boers had heard of the plan and reinforced the bridges with troops, the raids were called off. Lord Strathcona's Horse went to Durban instead, joining General Redvers Buller's army at Zandspruit on June 20.

Strathcona's Horse was soon actively engaged in a number of duties, including scouting, riding patrols, and taking part in raids and

Sam Steele proudly parades his men through downtown Ottawa (1900).

skirmishes as part of Buller's 3rd Mounted Brigade. It was during this time that Sam got to know Robert Baden-Powell, commander at the Siege of Mafeking, in which the British had held out for 217 days. As fellow cavalry officers, Steele and Baden-Powell met a number of times and grew to like and respect each other. They stayed in the field until October 14, then returned to Pretoria and a new round of duties. As always, Sam was fiercely proud of the work of his soldiers from the Canadian West.

As the Boers continued to wage a guerrilla-type war, the British command ordered that they were to be forcibly removed from their farms and taken to concentration camps for the duration of the conflict. Lord Strathcona's Horse was ordered to help with the seizing of Boer farms — a duty that did not sit well with Sam and his men, or any of the Canadians. Yet, products as they were of their time, they did not ask any questions.[18] Lieutenant E.W.B. Morrison, serving with a Royal Canadian Artillery battery, described his part in burning Boer Farms in November

Sam sits beside Lord Strathcona, his friend from his CPR days and the founder of Strathcona's Horse (1901).

1900: "... It was a terrible thing to see, and I don't know that I want to see another trip of the sort, but we could not help approving the policy, though it rather revolted most of us to be the instruments."[19]

On January 1, 1901, Sam received orders to prepare his men for the trip home to Canada. Their job was done. On their arrival in London on February 14, the men and officers of Strathcona's Horse were feted by London society and Lord Strathcona himself. The high point came when the regiment trooped to Buckingham Palace to receive the newly minted South African Medal.

All in all, Canada — and Sam — had done well. Very well indeed.

In 1901 Marie had a photo taken to send to Sam in South Africa. The girls are grown and are joined by brother Harwood who was born on May 5, 1887 (1901).

Sam, in the background, watches a photographer snap a picture of some of his men. As usual Sam manages to get into the picture (1900).

The Strathcona's mascot Peterboro Ben was not known for his good looks (1900).

Actions Undertaken by Strathcona's Horse in South Africa

June 20, 1900   Under command of General Buller's army, Lord Strathcona's Horse fights at Zanspruit, on the Transvaal border against Boer farmers fighting as Kommandos in a guerrilla campaign.

June 22, 1900   Lord Strathcona's Horse occupies the railway junction at Standerton.

July 4, 1900   Lord Strathcona's Horse arrives at Vlakfonte in their new base.

July 1900– August 1900   Acting as both scouts and an advance guard for allied troops, Lord Strathcona's Horse sees continuous action.

September 9 and 10, 1900   Sam and the Lord Strathcona's Horse attack a retreating column of Boers with huge success finally stopping at Spitzkop on September 25.

November 8, 1900   The Lord Strathcona's Horse conduct search and destroy sweeps clearing Boer fighters from the Buffelsdoorn Pass.

December 3, 1900   The Lord Strathcona's Horse fight at Good Hope farm. Sam describes it as an "... effective, coordinated operation."

January 6 and 8, 1901   The Lord Strathcona's Horse fight their last battle ambushing a group of Boer cavalry at Vet River.

THIRTEEN

South African Constabulary

THE

RIFLE SHOT'S MANUAL

—

H. SMITH

Sam kept a large library of military books. This was his personal copy of "The Rifle Shot's Manual" (1902).

Sam and Lord Baden Powell, the famed British General and founder of the Boy Scout movement, became fast friends in South Africa (1903).

The duties of Strathcona's Horse were done, but Sam was not done with South Africa. With his men safely back in Canada, he kept a promise he had made at Frederickstadt — to accept command of the B Division of the newly formed South African Constabulary (SAC).

Needing to ensure that he was not hurting his prospects in the future, Sam formally asked Prime Minister Wilfrid Laurier for permission to serve with the SAC, and was granted a five-year secondment. Sam then confirmed his colonelcy with his old friend, commander of the SAC Major General Robert Baden-Powell, before arranging a leave of absence from the NWMP. After a brief holiday in England, Sam embarked for the Cape in early June 1901. That same month he arrived at the temporary headquarters of the SAC at Modderfontein, north of Johannesburg.

The SAC, a total of ten thousand men and officers, was established to police the Transvaal and Orange River Colony. Sam's B Division was made up of six troops of experienced and hardened men.

As the war drew to a close in May 1902 the SAC turned from being a military force serving in the Boer War to being a true police force — one that Sam modeled on the NWMP. Just as in his days in western

Canada, Sam spent a great deal of his time keeping the peace between white (mostly Boer) and non-white (mostly African, with a strong Chinese minority) citizens in his territory. When not dealing with the citizens under his protection, Sam and the SAC looked after everything from delivering justice to animal husbandry.

Sam wearing the uniform of the South African Constabulary, a force he built based on the lessons he learned during his time with the NWMP (1903).

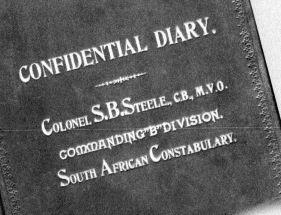

Sam's personal diary while he served with the South African Constabulary (1903).

CONFIDENTIAL DIARY.

Colonel S.B.Steele., C.B., M.V.O.

Commanding "B" Division.

South African Constabulary.

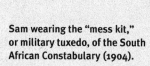

Sam wearing the "mess kit," or military tuxedo, of the South African Constabulary (1904).

Sam and Marie in South Africa (1906).

After years of time spent apart, Sam's wife and family joined Sam in South Africa on November 22, 1902. It was the beginning of a relatively long and happy time for the Steeles, with Sam playing the full role of colonel and attending with Marie all the best society events Pretoria had to offer.

When Baden-Powell was made Inspector General of Cavalry, he was replaced as commander of the SAC by Colonel John Nicholson. Sam was pleased to tell Nicholson that he "found the discipline [of the SAC] very good, and that the removal from the division of every man who had misbehaved himself in public or had been a disgrace to the corps, had a good effect, leaving the division with as fine and respectable a body of men as anyone could desire to command." Sam went on to report:

> I had found officers and men keen on their work and
> well acquainted with their districts and the inhabi-
> tants, and the officers with a sound knowledge of the

The Steele house, where Marie and Sam often entertained South African personalities including politicians and military leaders (1902).

character and capabilities of the N.C.O.'s and men under their command. They knew the country so well that they could take me over any by-path, trail or mountain to any place in the district. The officers and men were respected by the inhabitants of the country, all of whom made a practice of coming to them when they were in need of advice or help.[20]

With his five-year secondment drawing to a close, Sam announced in September 1906 that he was returning to Canada. His wife was growing increasingly ill as the Steeles and their children sailed for England on the steamship *Suevic* on October 7.

With Marie too ill to travel, Sam turned to his friend Frederick Borden to request a posting that allowed him to remain in England for the foreseeable future. Borden agreed and arranged for Sam to serve with Baden-Powell, who was in his last year as Inspector General of Cavalry.

A familiar sight — Sam riding his horse near his home (1903).

Occasionally, formal events required Sam to take a carriage rather than ride his favourite horse. There was no question that he preferred to ride (1903).

Sam's official duties were light, allowing him to spend a great deal of time with Marie and eventually nurse her back to health. For the balance of their time in England they, according to Sam, "visited every important battlefield, inspected the bottle dungeon of St. Andrew's, saw the golf course with its thousands of brave people, and, in fact, almost everything from Holyrood to the 'bore stone' and the home of the Fair Maid of Perth. We visited farms, castles, picture galleries and cathedrals, just the thing I liked."

In early 1907, Sir Frederick Borden visited London and the Steeles. Upon being assured that Marie was up to the long trip back to Canada, Borden offered Sam the command of Military District 13, with its headquarters in Calgary, Alberta. Sam was grateful for the opportunity to once again be in the command of soldiers, and Marie must have been happy for her husband, as she agreed to move her family once again.

Sam may have patterned the South Africn Constabulary on the NWMP, but there were differences, including men having pet monkeys (1904).

A formal invitation to a banquet in May 1904. Sam's duties often included dealing with politicians and the wealthy — a world Sam never really grew accustomed to.

The Mayor of Pretoria requests the honour of Colonel Steele's (O.C.S.A.C.) Company to a banquet to His Excellency the High Commissioner and the Members of the Inter-Colonial Council at the Grand Hotel. on Tuesday 31st May 1904. at 8 p.m.

R.S.V.P. to the Mayor's Secretary, P.O. Box 321. Pretoria.

FOURTEEN

Preparing Canada for War

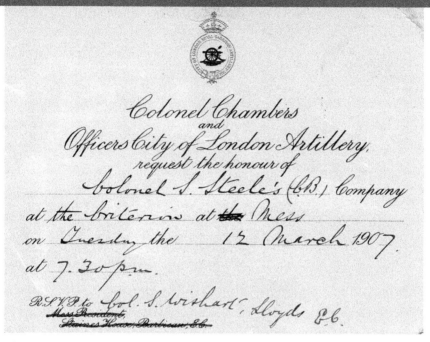

A formal invitation for Sam to attend the Officer Mess of the City of London Artillery (1907).

After brief stays in Montreal and Ottawa, Sam was in Calgary in July 1907 to take command of the training camp. Sam worked hard to build up the number and the skills of the men under his command. He, and others, felt that war in Europe was inevitable — the only question was when. Sam knew Canada would need well-trained troops, and he was determined to have them ready. In 1909, Ottawa asked Sam to go to Winnipeg to take command of Military District 10. For the next five years he worked at building up new units to prepare for the coming conflict in Europe.

Sam was particularly proud of the initiatives he spearheaded to improve the fitness and discipline of young people. He established an Army Cadet program that allowed boys to spend a week learning military drills and getting the physical training he felt many were missing.

Major and Mrs. Robert Belcher
request the honour of your presence
at the marriage of their daughter
Mary Northcote
to
Mr. Hugh Waldemar Nesbitt
on Wednesday, July the seventeenth
nineteen hundred and seven
at half past nine o'clock
Knox Church
Lethbridge, Alberta

In Lethbridge the Steeles attended the marriage of Major and Mrs. Belcher's daughter (1907).

A proud member of the Masons, Sam attended many of their events in Canada and England.

THE PLEASURE OF THE COMPANY OF

MR. *Col Steel*

IS REQUESTED AT ———— AND LADY

The First Annual Ball
UNDER THE AUSPICES OF THE

Ancient Free and Accepted Masons

OF CALGARY,

TO BE HELD IN

SHERMAN'S AUDITORIUM,

Friday Evening, May First
NINETEEN HUNDRED AND EIGHT

TICKETS $5.00. EXTRA LADIES $1.00.
DANCING AT 9 P.M.

W. F. W. LENT,
CHAIRMAN RECEPTION COMMITTEE.

R.S.V.P.
BRUCE ROBINSON,
HONORARY SECRETARY.

SURPLUS TO BE DONATED TO THE MASONIC HOME AND SCHOOL FUND

He drove the Manitoba government to include daily physical exercise in its school curriculum, a practice he was to see implemented across Canada. Sam also found time to take on the role of Commissioner of the Boy Scouts in Manitoba. During his tenure he had the pleasure of hosting, in Winnipeg, his old friend Baden-Powell — by then, a Lord — the founder of the Boy Scout Movement.

In addition, the sixty-three-year-old warrior had a busy social calendar due in part to the other roles that were expected of him. An honorary aide-de-camp to the governor general, he was also president of the Canadian South African Veterans' Association, the Winnipeg Canadian Club, and a branch of the Quebec Battlefields Association; in addition, he assisted thousands of ex-servicemen settle in western Canada. As a businessman, he was president of the Great Ibex and Slocan Mining Company and an administrator of the Strathcona Charitable Trust. He was in demand as a dinner speaker and kept an active schedule in support of various regiments and the Royal Northwest Mounted Police (RNWMP).

This was to be the last peaceful time the Steeles knew. War clouds were brewing over Europe and the world was about to become a very different, and dangerous, place.

As Sam continued his work in Winnipeg, a complex web of European treaties and alliances was slowly ensnaring the world. For years, Imperial

The officers and men of the 16th Light Horse in 1907.

6. Officers + 64. NCO's + men.   D. 16. L. Horse. 16 Aug 19

Germany and Great Britain had vied to be Europe's most powerful nation. Each was allied to other European nations: Britain to France and Russia; Germany to Austria-Hungary.

Sam stayed focused on his mission. Moving constantly throughout District 10, which stretched from the Alberta border to the Great Lakes, he pushed his officers to do better. He believed that the coming war would be a long and difficult one, and so he kept everyone in his command doing all they could in preparation.

When Archduke Ferdinand, heir to the Austro-Hungarian throne, was assassinated by a Serbian in June 1914, Austria-Hungary declared war on Serbia, and alliances quickly drew other nations into the conflict. Russia, bound to Serbia, rose to its defence. Germany, allied to Austria-Hungary,

The Steele house in Winnipeg in 1910. The house was torn down and an apartment block now stands in its place.

Sam prepares to review the men at Camp Sewell in Manitoba in 1911.

Sam and Lord Baden-Powell review a troop of Boy Scouts in Winnipeg in 1911.

Sam and Baden-Powell, the founder of the wordwide scouting movement, discuss the performance of the scouts being inspected (1911).

Baden-Powell reviews a troop of scouts in Winnipeg (1911).

declared war on Russia, forcing France and Great Britain, and their empires, to declare war on Germany. Ultimately, the war embraced the United States and the whole of Europe with the exception of Spain, Switzerland, the Netherlands, and the Scandinavian countries.

Joining the war was inevitable for Canada, a former colony of Great Britain. Many new Canadians had recently emigrated from Great Britain and felt the mother country's fight was naturally that of their new country, too. Across the nation, Canadians pledged support for the war effort. Former prime minister Sir Wilfrid Laurier summed up Canadian sentiment: "It is our duty to let Great Britain know and to let the friends and foes of Great Britain know that there is in Canada but one mind and one heart and that all Canadians are behind the Mother Country."[21]

Conservative prime minister Robert Borden, calling for a supreme national effort, offered Great Britain a full division, approximately twenty thousand men. The British government gratefully accepted the offer, and the call went out for volunteers to serve in the new Canadian Expeditionary Force.

Sam, with one eye on the coming war in Europe, had a lot to be proud of. He had built the militia force in District 10 from one thousand to six thousand men. Each had received the best training available. Sam felt his men were ready for war — and that he should be the one leading them into battle.

Soldiers receive a cup at Camp Sewell (1912).

16TH LIGHT HORSE

FOR KING AND EMPIRE

The Officers Commanding and 16th L.H. Chapter
Daughters of the Empire request the honor
of your Company at the
- Military - Ball -
At The Armoury, Grenfell,
On Thursday, the 30th January, 1913
At 8.30 o'clock p.m.

Colonel & Mrs. Steele

G. C. Neff, Secretary.

An answer is requested
Gentlemen $1.50.

Complimentary

Colonel and Mrs. Steele
spent a great amount
of time supporting the
troops by attending balls
and garden parties across
Alberta and Manitoba
(1913).

The Officer Commanding and Officers
of the 52nd Regiment, Prince Albert Volunteers
request the pleasure of your company at their
First Annual Ball
to be held in Harphill Hall
on Friday Evening, October Thirty-first
nineteen hundred and thirteen.

Prince Albert, Sask.
Dancing at 8.30

Urgent request for
R. S. V. P.
Captain A. I. Wilkinson

In 1913 Sam visited Prince
Albert, Saskatchewan,
and attended the
52nd Regiment, Prince
Albert Volunteers
Ball.

FIFTEEN

Sam Steele in the Great War

Sam at Camp Sewell in
Manitoba in 1914, just
before war with Germany
is declared.

In 1914 Sam was in Montreal preparing his troops for departure to Europe.

In 1914, Canada had a regular army of only 3,110 men and just a fledgling navy. Yet, in less than a month almost forty thousand men volunteered from all regions of the country, forcing Sam Hughes, minister of militia and defence, to temporarily suspend the recruitment drive.

Many young Canadians who rushed to local recruiting stations that August believed the war would be a great adventure. They confidently predicted that the conflict would be over by Christmas. In the patriotic fever sweeping the nation, no one foresaw the First World War dragging on for more than four bloody years and resulting in the death of some 20 million soldiers and civilians.

After basic selection, 32,000 recruits in the Canadian Expeditionary Force were dispatched on troop trains to Quebec for training. They were unquestionably patriotic, but most were civilians more familiar with pickaxes and ploughs than rifles and artillery. Before they saw action in the trenches of Europe, Canada's army needed to be trained and equipped.

When the question of who would lead the Canadian forces in Europe was discussed it was assumed that Sam Steele would be chosen — until Sam Hughes, the mercurial minister of militia and defence, stepped in. For reasons that are still unclear, Hughes wrote to Lord Frederick Roberts, an influential voice in the government in England, that "Steele was too old for the job … that Steele lacked the faculty of thinking and acting rapidly when the occasion might demand it."[22] When Sam heard about the comments he was incensed and waged a full-out letter-writing campaign to get Hughes to retract his comments.

Sam took Hughes's comments very personally. His personal correspondence is filled with references to how he was treated badly by Hughes and the media. He even wrote to his daughter Flora to tell her not to believe what the papers were saying. Sam enlisted everyone he

Senator Lougheed wrote Sam a personal letter congratulating him on his promotion to general (1914).

Sam took a moment in Montreal to get a photo taken — not in his familiar uniforms but in civilian clothes (1914).

could in the fight, including the brother of his old friend Frederick, Prime Minister Borden.

Abruptly, Hughes reversed his position. In December 1914, Hughes named Sam a major-general — the highest rank held by any Canadian. Sam also received the title of inspector general and was responsible for all training from the Great Lakes to the Pacific Ocean. Hughes assumed this would satisfy Sam and that he would give up on wanting to command in France. Sam protested that his experience made him the right choice to lead Canadian troops in France.

Hughes finally did an about-face and asked Sam if he would lead the 2nd Canadian Division, being recruited to be sent overseas. Sam did not hesitate. He immediately accepted the appointment and started planning for the mobilization of 25,000 Canadian troops for service in France.

Despite a broken left shoulder, suffered in a fall from a horse, Sam was in great spirits. He was returning to what he loved best — leading soldiers. But Sam was about to find out that for a major-general the greatest dangers were not necessarily on the battlefield.

Sam meeting with Field Marshal His Royal Highness the Prince Arthur, Duke of Connaught and Strathearn. The Duke of Connaught was the third son of Queen Victoria and the first member of the royal family to become governor general of Canada (1914).

M Y S E L F   <u>NOT</u>   G O D.   (by Sam)

"When Greek meets Greek" the battle's fair;
Kaiser and I ! gods ! what a pair!
For weapons we will choose ----Hot Air,
     I need no God.

Bill may be there with shot and shell,
His arms at first may fare quite well,
But, people, I can talk like Hell !
     I can by God.

That God created sun and rain
In seven days, is told in vain,
It took six weeks for me to train
     My men -- by God.

At my command my men arise,
Parade past me with right turned eyes,
These warriors --- mark you----symbolize
     Myself-- not God.

When, in Valcartier's latter days,
My Troops assembled 'neath my gaze
They merged each creed in one to praise
     Myself ---not God.

In language of poetic flow
I'll write my epitaph, you know,
(That's if I condescend to go
     Beneath the ôod)
My tombstone will need a P.T.O.
     So help me god.

Signed only as "Sam," this poem was authored by the general while he was in England (1915).

HEADQUARTERS
Shorncliffe Command.
28 JAN. 1915
SHORNCLIFFE

No. 19

The Bearer *General*
Major *S.B. Steele*
C.B., M.V.O
has permission to enter or
leave Dover Garrison at
any time.
H. D'aeth
Major,
D.A.A. & Q.M.G.

Signature of Holder.

S.B. Steele
Maj Gen

Sam's ID card to get
onto the Dover Garrison
(1915).

On March 20, 1915, Sam Hughes informed the British through Herbert Kitchener, British Secretary of War, "I propose appointing Major-General Sam Steele to command Second Canadian Overseas Division. He is splendid organizer and disciplinarian. Do you object?" Lord Kitchener's reply caught Hughes off-guard: "I am sorry that in the present state of warfare on the continent it would not be possible to place General Steele in command of a division. Very experienced commanders are necessary in such positions to do justice to the troops under their command."

Hughes roared back, "Regret your views Steele…. My opinion based on years of experience in war and manoeuvres convinces me that Steele and my brother, John Hughes, each as qualified as any officer in British service."

Kitchener, trying to placate an ally, replied, "I have no objection to General Steele coming here in contingent, if it is clearly understood by General Steele if the contingent takes the field as a division other arrangements will have to be made."

Despite his gaining Hughes's support, Sam's command of the 2nd Division and his

Sam, replete with walking stick, pauses for a minute at Shorncliffe (1915).

Sam, in the background, follows Field Marshal Herbert Kitchener (1915).

Sam stands in front of the CPR station in Winnipeg, circa 1915.

The family sits for a portrait in England. Sam had asked that Harwood, his son, be named his aide-de-camp. Harwood would become his father's greatest defender for the rest of his life (1916).

The classic pose of
Samuel Benfield Steele.

dreams of command in France and Belgium were doomed from the very start.

Sam consoled himself by throwing himself headlong into his work. He raised and trained his men, and in May 1915 brought to England 25,000 Canadians ready to fight. The Canadians were stationed at Shorncliffe Army Camp in Kent to receive their final training from British and Canadian combat veterans before heading across the English

Sam (right), with his signature western saddlebags hanging from his saddle, inspects the troops, 1916.

Channel. Sam's Canadians were known as the best trained and most fully prepared troops in the Empire.

The battle continued as to who would lead the 2nd Division in battle. Kitchener insisted that it would not be Sam and offered Hughes the pick of British major-generals. Hughes insisted that if Sam could not lead the 2nd Division, it would have to be another Canadian. Sam again took to recruiting friends in Canada and England to pressure Kitchener in his favour. It did not go well, and Kitchener announced in July 1915 that on August 17, R.E.W. Turner, a Boer war veteran, was to take command of the 2nd Division.

As a consolation prize, Sam was offered a position with the British Army as commander of all troops in the Shorncliffe area — both Canadian and British. Recognizing that if he had any hope of regaining command of "his" Canadians. it would be from England, he reluctantly accepted with the blessing of Hughes.

Sam became the patron of Perkins Bull Hospital in England and dedicated a large number of volunteer hours to the establishment (1916).

The last known portrait of Samuel Benfield Steele, 1918.

SIXTEEN

The End of a Legend

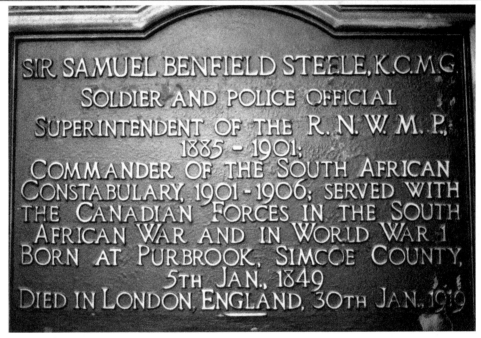

SIR SAMUEL BENFIELD STEELE, K.C.M.G.
SOLDIER AND POLICE OFFICIAL
SUPERINTENDENT OF THE R. N. W. M. P.,
1885 - 1901;
COMMANDER OF THE SOUTH AFRICAN
CONSTABULARY, 1901 - 1906; SERVED WITH
THE CANADIAN FORCES IN THE SOUTH
AFRICAN WAR AND IN WORLD WAR 1
BORN AT PURBROOK, SIMCOE COUNTY,
5TH JAN., 1849
DIED IN LONDON, ENGLAND, 30TH JAN., 1919

A plaque dedicated to Sam Steele's memory in his home town (1919).

From September 1915 until his retirement in July 1918, Sam's stellar military career foundered on the shoals of politics. Hughes, as indecisive and mercurial as always, ended up with three generals, all appointed by him, believing (justifiably) that they were commanding the Canadian troops in England.

It was confusing for allies and the troops — not to mention the generals themselves. When Prime Minister Borden received intense pressure to resolve the matter, he fired Hughes, leaving Sam in the worst possible position. Sam had lost his protector in Hughes and, worse, was seen as part of the problem. The Canadian government pressed Sam to retire — even threatening his pension if he continued to serve with the British. Finally, even Sam could not withstand the pressure and accepted his retirement in July 1918.

Sam Steele's grave in the cemetery at St. John's Anglican Cathedral in Winnipeg, Manitoba.

An honour guard carries the casket holding the body of Sam Steele (1919).

In the end, Sam Steele did not get to command Canadian troops in the field. He was not even allowed the honour of seeing the war out as a soldier on active duty.

Someone once wrote that old soldiers just fade away. Not so with Samuel Benfield Steele.

After his retirement, Sam moved his family to the London suburb of Putney on the southwest bank of the Thames. There he started to plan his return to western Canada, so he could live out his retirement with his family in the part of the world he loved so much. Sam also reported that he had caught a cold.

As his cold grew worse, Sam got word that he would have to wait in London, as front-line troops had first priority on the limited number of ships sailing to Canada. He thought nothing of the delays and prepared to enjoy his last days in England. Soon, however, Sam was confined to his bed. The man who had kept a daily diary all his life wrote his last entry on November 30, 1918 — too sick to write any more.

On January 30, 1919, Samuel Benfield Steele slipped into a coma and died. The great man had fallen victim to Spanish influenza, as had millions of others in the worldwide epidemic. Sam's death at age seventy marked the end of an era.

A charger with a pair of cavalry boots backwards in the stirrups, a long tradition at the death of a cavalry officer (1919).

Crowds lined the route to the cemetery as pipers escorted Sam's casket.

The gun caisson, flanked by RNWMP officers, carrying Sam to his final resting place.

Even little children came out to say goodbye to "Colonel Sam."

Back side of Sam Steele's grave marker.

DEO, REGI ET PATRIA

Sam had been determined that his body be buried in Winnipeg, but again he would have to wait — there was no room for his casket on any the ships still ferrying thousands of troops home.

On February 1, 1919, Sam's Union Jack–draped casket was loaded on a gun carriage and carried through the streets of London. Sam would have been proud, for accompanying him on his last trip were a troop of Royal North West Mounted Police, a troop of Lord Strathcona's Horse dressed in their Boer War uniforms, and hundreds of men from the 2nd Canadian Division.

For the next four months Sam's body was kept in cold storage, waiting as the living returned to Canada. In July there was finally room for Sam Steele on a ship for the long voyage home. The Canadian Pacific Railway, which also operated a shipping line, offered to bring Sam home for free. After all, he was an old friend of the company.

Sam's body finally arrived in Winnipeg, just in time for the General Strike of 1919. Police officers, including members of the RNWMP, were in pitched battles with strikers, who were demanding better working conditions. Rioters controlled the streets. But when the mayor of Winnipeg asked for time to bury the old policeman and military general, the strikers quietly agreed. Many attended the service and procession to St. John's Cemetery, alongside dignitaries that included cabinet members and high-ranking military officers.

Perhaps George Hope Johnston, a rancher and former policeman who knew Sam well, described Sam the best:

> He had all the requisites of a pioneer chief — a commanding presence, absolute fearlessness and a wonderful control over all sorts and conditions of men.... An officer of magnificent physique ... in his tall, powerful figure, deep-chested proportions and massive soldiers, he suggested prodigious strength ... erect as a pine tree and limber as a cat, he would have been remarked in any company ... he was feared and respected by men who as a usual thing feared neither God nor man. When an occasion arose for a rapid decision, he never waited a moment; and when he struck, he struck hard.[23]

The official death certificate for Sam Steele. While the certificate clearly says Sam died of diabetes, his son Harwood would always say his father died of complications of the flu. Harwood believed that admitting his father died of a disease like diabetes somehow diminished Sam's legend.

GENERAL SAM B. STEELE, C.B., M.V.O, A.D.C.

General Sam B. Steele, C.B., M.V.O., A.D.C., formerly inspector general of Canadian western forces, died today in England. He was one of Canada's best known soldiers, holding the medals of the Red River Expedition of 1874 of the Northwest Rebellion of 1885, and of the South African war. In the Northwest rebellion he was mentioned in despatches, and his work in South Africa was noted in the same way three times during the operations in Natal and the Transvaal, and twice in the Orange River country. For his South African services, besides the Queen's medal and 4 clasps, and the King's medal with 2 clasps, he was specially mentioned by Lord Kitchener and was honored by being gazetted an honorary lieutenant-colonel in the British army.

Sam's obituary (1919).

Contd.

Noted Canadian Officer Passed Away at Putney Following Two Months Illness

Went Overseas in 1915 as Commander of Second Division— Had Distinguished Career

London, Jan. 30. — General Sam Steele, K.C.M.G., died at Putney, London, today. He had been ill about two months, but the end came rather suddenly. General Steele was one of Canada's best known military men. He was born in Simcoe county, Ontario, in 1849, and began his military career in the 35th battalion, Simcoe Foresters, in 1869. After qualifying at Toronto Military college he served through the Red River revellion in 1871. He later joined the Northwest Mounted Police as a sergeant-major. He commanded the cavalry scouts in the Northwest rebellion of 1885. He quelled the Kootenay trouble in 1887.

In South Africa.

In the South African war he commanded the Strathcona Horse and was mentioned in the despatches of Lord Kitchener and Sir Redvers Buller and received the Order of the Commander of the Bath and became a member of the Victorian order. In 1915 he was made inspector-general of the forces in western Canada, going overseas as commander of the second Canadian division. He commanded afterwards the Imperial and Canadian troops at Shorncliffe.

The late Gen. Steele's son, Harold Steele, is at present serving with the British imperial army, in which he holds captain's rank. For conspicuous services on the battlefield he has received the Military Cross and has been mentioned in despatches. Recently he was granted leave of absence to complete a book which he is writing on the war. A couple of years ago he issued a book of verse on war and other themes, which was favorably received.

NO FINER RECORD IN WHOLE DOMINION

Few Canadians have a prouder military record than Major-General Samuel Beneld Steele, K.C.M.G., C.B., M.V.O., who has just passed away. In the Dominion his name is a household word.

Although nearly seventy years of age and holding the important war administrative post of inspector-general of western forces when war broke out, he resigned his job in February, 1915, to go overseas as general commanding the Second Canadian division. His force arrived in England in April, 1915, and he commanded it there at Shorncliffe until it went to France in September of that year, when it was found necessary to replace him with a younger man.

Then the late general was given command of the Shorncliffe military ..., ... held until early this year, when failing health forced his resignation. He has remained in England, feeling that he could not tear himself away from proximity to the great tragedy from which advancing years had forced his participation.

News of the death of General Steele will stir deep regret throughout Canada, particularly in Winnipeg, with the military life of which city he has been closely associated for almost half a century.

In Early Days.

Colonel "Sam" Steele, as he was best known here, was a soldier by breeding, early associations, and long and distinguished service. A disciplinarian without being a martinet, he was respected without being feared by the men under his command, whether these were constables of the Royal North West Mounted police; cowboys enlisted without much actual training for service in the Alberta Field force, under the command of Major-General T. D. Strange for the suppression of the second Riel rebellion in 1885; or that now famous force raised by General Steele and equipped and armed by the late Lord Strathcona, known to fame as the Strathcona Horse, for the South African war in 1899.

His father, Capt. Elmes Steele, R.N., was a midshipman on board the Leopard in 1807, when that vessel fired on the Chesapeake to enforce the right to search, the claim to enforce which by Great Britain, led to the war of 1812 with the United States. After leaving the navy Captain Steele was given land grants in County Simcoe, for which county he sat as member from 1841 to 1844.

In South African War.

His work in South Africa was at first in command of Lord Strathcona's Horse, for which he was mentioned in despatches by Lord Kitchener, and Gen. Sir Redvers Buller on no less than five occasions, as also by Field-Marshal Lord Roberts. For these services he received promotion, the Queen's medal with three clasps, th

Order of Commander of the Bath and member of the Victoria Order.

Upon the conclusion of the war he reorganized the South African constabulary, which he commanded during the remainder of his stay in South Africa, suppressed Chinese outrages on the Rand, and disarmed the natives of the North Transvaal, who, under Chief Sekukuni, were causing much trouble.

Upon his return to Canada in 1907, he was given the command of Military District 13, with headquarters at Calgary, from which place he was transferred to Winnipeg in command of Military District 10.

Early in 1915, Colonel Steele was sent to England with the rank of major-general in command of Canadian units in England, with headquarters at Folkestone.

General Steele hoped to get a command in France, but possibly his age stood in his way.

Born in Ontario.

Gen. Steele was born in Simcoe county, at Purbrook, and qualified in a long course of artillery under Sir George French, R.A., one of the leading artillerymen of the time. His strenuous life had left but little mark upon him. He came of a fighting family. His father, Captain Elmes Steele, R.N., sat for Simcoe in the old Canadian assembly during 1841-1844, and was actively engaged in the wars of Great Britain up to 1815. Two of the general's uncles were also in the navy. Tom was killed in battle. Edward was drowned in the Baltic when in command of a battleship at the age of 28.

He was married in 1890 to Marie Elizabeth, eldest daughter of the late Robert Harwood, M.P., and had three children, two girls and a boy.

Was a Sergeant-Major.

"Sam" Steele served in the Red River expedition under the late field marshal, then Sir Garnet Wolseley, in 1870, in which expedition Sir Redvers Buller was also an officer. Joining the North West Mounted police in 1873 as sergeant-major of the force, under Col. French, he took part in the march of that famous body, then only 300 strong, from Winnipeg to the Rocky Mountains. Steele was the first and last sergeant-major of the whole force, that rank being done away with when he received his commission as inspector.

General Steele was known and trusted implicitly by Sir John Macdonald, who when he held the reins of government in Canada always kept the control of the mounted police in his own hands.

When it was necessary to select an officer of the mounted police to ensure that law and order were observed during the construction of the C. P. R. through eastern British Columbai, it was Inspector Steele who was selected by Sir John Macdonald for the post, which in those early days was no sinecure. The Northern Pacific had been completed during the previous year, and all the murderers, gamblers and hard cases who had flouted all authority in Montana and Idaho, flocked to British Columbia, hoping to continue their evil courses there.

How speedily they were undeceived those who were on the road during construction will well remember.

Part in Riel Rebellion

When the Riel rebellion broke out in April, 1885, Steele was at once ordered to report in Calgary with all the men under his command and, with the rank of major, in a few weeks he organized, mounted and drilled a complete force of police and cowboys, which, with the 65th battalion from Montreal and other troops, afterwards did such effective service under General Strange, defeating Big Bear, the Cree chief, at Loon lake.

When the gold rush to the Yukon was at its height in 1898, Superintendent Steele was sent there from Macleod, where he was in command of two divisions of the Royal Northwest Mounted Police, and where he repeated on a still larger scale his work of 1884-85 in British Columbia. In addition to his duties as police officer in command in the Yukon, he was also a member of the council there, and in that capacity rendered invaluable service to the government.

Epilogue
Sam Steele's Legacy

Sam Steele was truly a product of his times. He was a rough and tough hunter and sportsman, a consummate soldier, and the very embodiment of the law in Canada and South Africa.

Steele had his weaknesses. He was always short of funds — the result of being born poor in a world of rich officers and politicians. Living up to the image of Sam Steele cost money. However, Sam Steele, the man, was friend to many and enemy of almost no one. Fellow police officers and soldiers, settlers in the West, First Nations peoples, and Canadians in general liked and respected "the Colonel."

Steele left a legacy of strength and courage, a legacy of fairness and justice. Canada would miss Samuel Benfield Steele — there would never be another like him.

Notes and Credits

Notes

1. Samuel Benfield Steele, *Forty Years in Canada: Reminiscences of the Great Northwest, With Some Account of his Service in South Africa* (Toronto: McClelland, Goodchild and Stewart, 1915).
2. Canadian Parliamentary Bill establishing the NWMP Section 13, May 20, 1873.
3. Ibid.
4. R.G. MacBeth, *Policing the Plains: Being the Real Life Record of the Famous Royal North-West Mounted Police* (Toronto: Hodder & Stoughton, 1921).
5. Steele, *Forty Years in Canada*.
6. Ibid.
7. Captain Ernest J. Chambers, *The Royal North-West Mounted Police: A Corps History* (Montreal: The Mortimer Press, 1906).
8. Steele, *Forty Years in Canada*.
9. Ibid.
10. Ibid.
11. "Treaties," Blackfoot Crossing Historical Park, www.blackfoot-crossing.ca/treaties.html.
12. Pierre Burton, *The Last Spike: The Great Railway, 1881–1885* (Toronto: McClelland & Stewart, 1971).
13. Steele, *Forty Years in Canada*.
14. Ibid.
15. Ibid.
16. Ibid.
17. Ibid.

18. Corporal Ivor Edward Cecil Rice-Jones, Diary, August 31, 1900, Corporal Ivor Edward Cecil Rice-Jones papers, M1037, GMA; Militia Order 26, February 1, 1900, Boer War collection, M6 6 F1, Provincial Archives of Manitoba, Winnipeg.

19. Doctor Chris Madsen, "Canadian Troops and Farm Burning in the South African War," *Canadian Military Journal* 6, no. 2 (Summer 2005), http://www.journal.forces.gc.ca/vo6/no2/history -histoire-eng.asp.

20. Steele, *Forty Years in Canada.*

21. Canada, *Debates,* House of Commons, 12th Parliament, 4th Session [Special War Session], vol. 117, August 18, 1914, http://parl .canadiana.ca/view/oop.debates_HOC1204_01.

22. G.W.L. Nicholson, *Canadian Expeditionary Force: The Official History of the Canadian Army in the First World War* (Ottawa: The Queen's Printer, 1962), 112.

23. Captain Elmes Steele, R.M. and Major-General Sir S.B. Steele, *A Medonte Pioneer and His Famous Son* (Orillia, ON: Orillia Historical Society and the University of Toronto, 1954).

Credits

Images used with permission.

Bruce Peel Special Collections Library, University of Alberta: 9, 18, 20, 26, 33, 41, 42, 44, 45 (top), 45 (bottom), 47, 48–49, 50, 51, 52 (top), 52 (bottom), 53 (top), 53 (bottom), 54, 55, 56, 57 (left), 57 (right), 58–59, 60 (top), 60 (bottom), 61, 62, 63, 64, 65, 66, 67, 68–69, 70, 71, 72, 73, 74–75, 76, 77 (top), 77 (bottom), 78, 79, 80–81, 82 (top), 82 (bottom), 83, 85 (top), 85 (bottom), 86, 87, 88, 89, 90, 92–93, 94–95, 96, 97, 98, 99 (top), 99 (bottom), 101, 102, 103, 104 (top), 104 (bottom), 105, 106, 107, 108, 109 (top), 109 (bottom), 110, 111 (top), 111 (bottom), 112, 113 (top), 113 (middle), 113 (bottom), 115, 166 (top), 116 (bottom), 113 (top), 113 (bottom), 117, 118, 119 (top), 119 (bottom), 120, 121, 122 (top), 122 (bottom), 123 (top), 123 (bottom), 124, 125, 126, 127, 128, 129, 130, 131, 132 (top), 132 (bottom), 133 (top), 133 (bottom), 134, 135, 136, 137, 138; Orillia Museum of Art and History: 15, 16, 17 (top), 17 (bottom), 19 (bottom), 25 (bottom)

All other images are in the public domain.

ALSO BY NORMAN S. LEACH

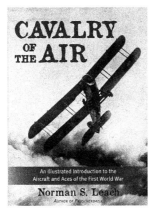

Cavalry of the Air

Many of the airmen of the First World War who challenged both the enemy and death did not survive. In the clinging mud and trench warfare of the First World War, it was soon clear that the cavalry — the elite of the elite — would be of little use.

The dashing men and officers of the cavalry searched for a way to be front and center in the conflict, and found it in the new air forces being established on both sides of the Western Front. Soon lances and sabres were replaced by silk scarves and machine guns. Combat on horseback was replaced by dogfights in the air — one-on-one and in great flying formations — always between warriors. No technology changed more in the five years of the war, and none would have a bigger impact.

From Great Britain to Canada to Australia and New Zealand, new heroes took the honour and dash of the cavalry to the air in flying machines — which would change the face of war forever.

Though storytelling, period and contemporary photos and the words of the flying aces themselves, *Cavalry of the Air* brings the history of First World War air combat to life.